The Yorkshire Ouse Walk

Ivan E Broadhead

Meridian Books

Published 2009 by Meridian Books

© Ivan E Broadhead 2009

ISBN 978-1-869922-59-7

Meridian Books
8 Hartside Close, Lutley, Halesowen, West Midlands B63 1HP

Printed in Great Britain by Cromwell Press Group,
Trowbridge, Wiltshire

Dedicated to Katie Joanne
and
Charlotte Rose

Contents

Introduction 7
Routes 10
Maps 10
Towpaths 10
Useful Websites and Phone Numbers 11

Acknowledgments 12

1 Waif of the Workhouse 13
Ouseburn to Newton on Ouse 13
    Saga Of The Lock 22

2 Femmes Fatales 25
Newton on Ouse to Rawcliffe Ings 25
    Murder Most Foul 29
    Merry Nuns Of Monkton 31
    The Quest For Speed 34

3 Double Jeopardy 35
Rawcliffe Ings to Skeldergate Bridge 35
    In Memoriam 38
    Bridge Fever 45

4 On Sacred Soil 48
Skeldergate Bridge to Naburn 48
    Beating the Bounds 59

5 Sources of Sadness 61
Naburn to Cawood 61
    Scandal and Sleaze 65
    Christmas Carollers Tragedy 68
    Humpty Dumpty Slept Here 70

6 Devoted Duo 73
Cawood Bridge to Selby Bridge 73
    Follies Of Infatuation 75
    Mind Of A Monk 81

7 Fallacies Exposed 83
Selby to Hemingbrough 83
    Small Link in Big Chain 84
    Divine Right 91

8 Marriage of Waters 92
Hemingbrough to Boothferry 92
    Studies in Success 98

9   Bartholomew's Vineyard 102
      Boothferry to Swinefleet. *102*
        Rags to Riches. 106
        Tale of Tom Puddings. 113
10   Time and Tide 115
      Swinefleet to Adlingfleet Ings *115*
        Refuge for Royalty? 124

Illustrations

Pleasure cruiser passing Blue Bridge (Walk 4). 8

Old Goole (Walk 10) 9

Old workhouse alongside York-Borougbridge road . 14

Ornamental source stone 15

Stone at Gt Ouseburn 16

Fingerpost at Gt Ouseburn 17

Aldwark toll bridge. 18

Cruisers on River Ouse above Linton Lock 21

The Newton on Ouse Landing. 25

Cruisers at Nidd Mouth 27

Scarborough Railway Bridge 39

Pleasure Craft at Marygate Landing 40

Lendal Bridge 41

Remains of St Mary's Abbey. 45

Official flood marker. 46

Ornate lamp on Skeldergate Bridge 46

Skeldergate Bridge 47

Bishops Wharf. 48

The River Foss flood barrier 49

The Millennium Bridge 50

Fulford Hall across the River Ouse. 51

Bishopthorpe Palace overlooking the River Ouse . . 52

Cawood Bridge 61

Naburn Weir, marking the tidal limit of the Ouse . . 63
The carollers' gravestone 66
Stillingfleet church and the carollers' gravestone . . . 67
The gatehouse of Cawood Castle 69
Naburn Marina 72
The Grey Horse and Main Street, Kelfield 77
Plaque marking the former pinfold in Kelfield 77
Selby Abbey 78
Selby Market Cross, adjacent to the Abbey 79
Hemingbrough Church spire 84
One of the bench ends in Hemingbrough Church . . 86
Another bench end 86
Misericord in Hemingborough Church 87
The Airmyn clock tower 95
Carved bench ends in Drax church 97
Bell and clock on Drax school 98
More carved bench ends 99
Aerial view of Howden Dyke 103
Howden Market Square 104
Memorial to Sailors on the river bank at Goole . . . 108
Commemorative plate showing the Goole Coat of Arms 109
The 'Tom Pudding' barge system 111
Unloading cargo vessels in Goole docks 114
The clock on Whitgift church 117
Lighthouse at Ousefleet 118
The Hope & Anchor Inn at Blacktoft 122

Introduction
River of Destiny

In *Striding Through Yorkshire*' A J Brown says the 'Ouse is one of the greatest rivers of England. To a Yorkshireman it is the greatest, since it derives from a fusion of all the chief rivers of the shire. Gone are the wild songs of the mountains and the tumult of the falls ... but (in the Ouse) there is a smoothness that conceals strength.'

From as far back as the Roman invasion of Britain, and probably long before that fateful day, the Yorkshire Ouse has attracted, baffled and bewildered men, earning both respect and curses from those who have ventured on its unpredictable waters or lived near its banks

For many centuries the river was known as 'The Ouse' or even 'Northern Ouse' to distinguish it from its brother of the same name that straddles Buckinghamshire, Bedfordshire, Huntingdonshire, Cambridgeshire, and Norfolk before discharging itself into the Wash.

The Yorkshire Ouse also discharges its waters into the North Sea, but before uniting with the River Trent to pour out through their common estuary – The Humber – it twists and turns touching practically every point of the compass.

From its humble beginnings it winds about 60 miles(almost 100km) through the Vale of York – a fertile thousand-square-mile lowland oasis bounded by the Pennines on the west, the Wolds to the east, and moors in the north – before plunging into the Humber at around 3,500 cubic feet a second. On the way it swallows up lesser streams from picturesque dales – the Ure, Swale, Nidd, Wharfe, Aire and Derwent, as well as the tiny Foss and the rumbling Don.

This is a peculiar river because its width constantly varies from well over 1,500 feet at Trent Falls to a little more than 100 feet at Naburn. All of this is a tidal section in which there are at least thirty narrow bends with deep channels scoured on the outside and shoals built up on the inside. For the tides are by no means insignificant, flooding in with a fierce rush possibly unequalled by any other river in England. The flood tide averages about 6 knots, bringing about 17 feet of water at Goole and 10 feet at Naburn Lock.

The whole outfall of the Ouse, Trent and Humber formed a vast tidal inlet like the Wash at one period in the remote past. As a result

*Pleasure cruiser passing Blue Bridge over the confluence of the River Foss
with the River Ouse (Walk 4)*

successive invaders swept far inland and established permanent
settlements at York, which for centuries was a flourishing port.
Thirteenth and fourteenth-century merchants were handling cargoes of
stone, timber, wine, spices, salt, linen, lead and coal as well as woad
and madder, clapboard and wainscots, whose very names sound
strange to us now. Tar and pitch from the coalfields of the West Riding
as well as barley, flax and other agricultural products went down the
Ouse to the Humber. Undoubtedly the most common craft carrying
these cargoes was the Yorkshire or Humber keel, a vessel to the Ouse
what the Trow was to the Severn or the Spritsail Thames barge to
London's river. These distinctive, flat-bottomed, shallow-draught,
single-masted, square-sailed craft, claimed by some people to be direct
descendants of Viking vessels which once plagued the locality, were
products of boatyards at Selby, Cawood, Fulford, Naburn and
Stillingfleet. From the thirteenth century the merchants of Hull began to
monopolize the sea trade, and then the canal age was born, creating
new ports like Goole. The railway age came on its heels, depriving the

Ouse still further of the merchandise which had been borne on this fluid highway to the Humber ports.

The Rivers Ouse and Foss Navigation Trust, made up of York city councillors, was set up in 1727 and control was not relinquished until October 1989 when the British Waterways Board took over responsibility – a switch officially recognised six months later on 9 April 1990.

However, the Ouse is still a viable navigation, living up to the proud boast that it carries more cargoes further inland than any other in Britain, and nowhere do ships from the high seas penetrate further from salt water than they do at Selby. There appears to be universal acceptance too of the view that the river is a great asset for all to share and enjoy.

This book aims to reaffirm and endorse that vision.

I've seen rapid Severn careering along,
And dark flowing Thames, the majestic and strong,
The Cam, and the Isis, those haunts of the muse,
But to me none surpass the fair banks of the Ouse.

Anon

Old Goole (Walk 10)

Routes

All the routes, except when on roads, follow paths that, so far as we are aware, are public rights of way or are permissive paths (such permission can be withdrawn but that would usually be unlikely). Every effort has been made to ensure that descriptions are correct and the routes have been carefully checked. However, no guarantee can be given that they are error free and that there are no misprints or inaccuracies.

As the route in the main follows either the flood protection barrier or the river embankment, the path could be impassable at times of flooding and even for a while after the floods subside (due to debris), so do not walk on this route at these periods.

No serious problems of access were encountered on any of the route Sometimes the route goes through gardens that lead onto the flood barrier – please be respectful of their property. In some places, there could be cattle/sheep grazing. where the Environment Agency has let their land to farmers or where farmland leads up to the flood barrier. Please follow the country code by not frightening the animals and by securing gates. Dogs should be kept on a leash.

No obstructions were found on the paths. However, if you do encounter any obstructions on rights of way please report them to the Rights of Way section of the local authority.

Be aware that some sections of the route, especially at the lower end of the Ouse, are not regularly walked, so the path can be overgrown.

Maps

The sketch maps are intended as a guide, not to replace Ordnance Survey maps which, together with a compass and some basic first aid, you should always have with you. Although we hope this will not happen, there is always the possibility that you might need to change your route because of bad weather or some unexpected incident. Maps should preferably be the Explorer series which are much more useful to walkers than Landrangers.

Towpaths

Few towpaths are rights of way but British Waterways permits, and indeed usually encourages, their use by walkers and cyclists. It does mean, however, that when a towpath is closed for work on the waterway there may be no diversion, such as is generally provided by the local authority when a right of way has to be closed. Another good reason why you should always have map and compass with you.

Useful Websites and Phone Numbers

Floodline: This provides information about flooding and threats of flooding. However, the absence of flooding on roads and in residential areas does not mean that footpaths are clear.

www.environment-agency.gov.uk/subjects/flood/floodwarning

phone: 0845 988 1188

Rail enquiries:

www.nationalrail.co.uk

phone: 08457 484950

All forms of public transport:

www.traveline.org.uk

phone: 0870 6082608

Business information (useful for taxi phone numbers):

www.scoot.co.uk

Maps: www.streetmap.co.uk

River information:

www.britishwaterways.co.uk

The Ramblers' Association:

www.ramblers.org.uk

www.communigate.co.uk/york/yorkramblers2

Local Authorities and Rights of Way

York: www.york.gov.uk 01904 613161

Selby www.selby.gov.uk 01757 705101

Goole www.goole.gov.uk 01405 763652

Acknowledgments

I nspiration and enthusiastic help towards preparing this book has come from numerous sources who in addition to providing valuable historical and other information, giving detailed directions, patiently indulging naïve curiosity, have offered useful suggestions, and whole-heartedly helped in other ways to fill gaps in my knowledge.

Amongst these must be included library staffs in and around York, especially York Reference Library, and officials of British Waterways, Goole Town Council, York City Council, Selby District Council, The Environment Agency, as well as innumerable and unnamed acquaintances against whose unsuspecting minds have been sharpened many thoughts and phrases which appear in these pages and to whom I owe a debt of gratitude.

Acknowledgment is also due to all those whose contribution was both immediate and tangible, thus helping to speed the book to publication and ultimately into your hands, dear reader.

One person's efforts who must not go unmentioned are those of Shelagh Martin who walked every inch of the route – as well as possible variations – and made practical observations. To her my unqualified gratitude.

Finally, without the endless patience, tolerance, encouragement and unqualified support of our respective spouses who make anything seem possible and enable much to be actual,this book would never have emerged.

Every possible care has been taken to ensure accuracy but if there is any errors or omissions then the responsibility is mine alone.

Ivan E Broadhead
York 2008

1

Waif of the Workhouse

Ouseburn to Newton on Ouse

> **Start:** Campbell & Penty warehouse B6265 (Grid Ref 436618).
> **Distance:** Approx 7 miles/ 11 Kilometres.
> **Terrain:** Road and river embankment.
> **Maps:** Explorer 299; Landranger 99/100.
> **Car Parking:** Lay-by on both sides of B6265 north of warehouse.
> **Public Transport:** 142/3 Bus from York to Ripon via Gt Ouseburn (Harrogate Coach Travel 01423 339600).
> **Refreshments:** The Crown Inn, Great Ouseburn; College Arms, Linton; Blacksmiths Arms and Dawnay Arms, Newton on Ouse.

Conveniently, there are substantial parking lay-bys on both sides of the B6265 just about 300 yards (250 metres) north of the Campbell & Penty Warehouse, which is the start of our walk. Turn down Carr Side Road at the side of the warehouse and go into Great Ouseburn before engaging with the river itself. ➔ *page 16*

Just north of Little Ouseburn village on the right hand side of the great road called Dere Street which linked the Roman legions in Eboracum- York and Aldborough – Isurium, near Boroughbridge and is now B6265, stands a former workhouse building which since 1950 when it was sold for £2,700, has served as a warehouse for corn and seed merchants Campbell & Penty.

Erected in 1854 the complex of buildings and gardens covers about four acres and was built as a workhouse to serve some forty-two townships which came under the jurisdiction of the Great Ouseburn Poor Law Union Board of Guardians. Opposite is Moor Lane along which legend has it inmates carried stone they had broken for repair of the Great North Road.

In its time it held thousands of destitute folk, itinerant labourers, unwed pregnant women, and gave a night's shelter to great numbers of vagrants. However they were not always as grateful as might be expected according to a March 11, 1906 report from York Police Court when five inmates were charged with refusing to do their allotted task work. Samuel Shaw, assistant taskmaster said that at 8.00am he asked

Old workhouse alongside York-Borougbridge road

the five men, along with about 30 others in the casual ward to go and do their morning's work.

The five men in court refused and after being asked several times the master was called.

One of the five said they entered the workhouse the previous night and the place was not fit for a dog to live in. He had a piece of dry bread and some cold water given to him and put in a cold place where there was no fire. He wanted warm water and would have worked had he got it. Apparently five ounces of very good bread was allowed each inmate and a short time after the complaint the hot water was ready. The Bench said they wanted to deal leniently with the men, although they

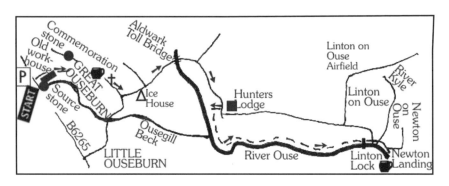

Ornamental source stone

were liable to a month's imprisonment, they would be sent to prison for one day.

Standing in the grounds, somewhat obscured from the road when trees are in leaf, is an ornamental stone column about 12 feet high which marks the source of the River Ouse. Inscribed on one face is the legend, 'Ouse River Head' and on others, 'Ouse Gill Spring Ft., York 13 miles, Boroughbridge 4 miles'. Unclear is whether this weatherbeaten grey stone column was erected primarily as a mileage gauge on this important turnpike route and a reminder of the historic waters born here, or a celebration of the river source and a functional afterthought. Antiquarian and historian William Camden whose Britannia appeared in 1586 described Ouse Gill Beck as 'the pretty little rivulet which runs into the river at Ouseburn giving the name to the Ouse and robbing the Eure of it'.

Starting from Ure Head on Abbotside Common the River Ure runs for 68 miles through Wensleydale and is swelled by a number of minor tributaries and one major one – the River Swale which joins it from the left just downstream of Boroughbridge before its confluence with Ouse Gill Beck and the change of identity.

The River Ouse appears originally to have had two British names; it was called Uys and the Ewi. Both names, however, signify nothing more noteworthy than water in general, and it seems likely that for *some time, when names were less regularised than today, it was known by the two different names in different localities. Occasionally it might be called by both conjoined, which ultimately became compounded into Isur, then Isurium. Over the years this word was corrupted to the Roman Isis, and later the Saxon, Ouse. Both historian John Leland, who visited York circa 1539, and William Camden agree in the view that the river was called Ure, Eure, or Youre and that the Saxons added the termination 'wic' make Eurewic – a place of strength and retreat – from which in the course of time came our Ouse.*

Towards the end of the twelfth century William de Stuteville, Lord of Knaresborough, gave all his lands hereabouts, together with his body, to Fountains Abbey. It was the same William de Stuteville somewhere about 1190 who made the ditch for Ouse Gill Beck which separates the two villages of Great and Little Ouseburn.

Barely four miles long, the willow-lined Ouse Gill Beck meanders towards its bigger brother. This then is the birthplace of the River Ouse – a waterway as historic, as scenic and as significant in our history as the Thames.

After about two thirds of a mile (1km) you reach an intersection where opposite is a small green on which sits a boulder mounted on a stone plinth marking the boundary between Branton Green and Great Ouseburn. Inscribed around the base is a quotation from Romeo & Juliet Act 3 Scene 5:

'I HAVE MORE CARE TO STAY THAN WILL TO GO'.

Turn right to pass the old West Riding fingerpost, inscribed *Yorks W.R.* which shows distances with fractions of a mile.

Walk down Main Street, Great Ouseburn where seventeenth century cottages intermingle with modern detached houses. Go forward past *The Crown Inn* on your right. Further along on your left you pass the church dedicated to St Mary the Virgin. ➜*page 17*

Stone at Gt Ouseburn

Fingerpost erected by former West Riding County Council at Gt Ouseburn

The church has belfry windows divided by shafts, a Norman slit in one wall, a thirteenth-century lancet in another and later battlements. Unlike most of the benefactors of yesteryear who, according to various boards and tablets, left cash for one charitable cause or another, Mr William Henlock who died on 16th September 1866 left to the village poor the interest on £200 invested in Consolidated 3 per cent Annuities – a fact inscribed on a stark memorial on an inside wall.

Yeoman's Cottage also on your left with the legend 'Anno Dom 1637 R:T' over the doorway testifies to its great age.

After about two-thirds of a mile (1km) from the Green turn left into Boat Lane to walk to Aldwark toll bridge. ➜ *page 18*

Just past the 'Old Lodge', on the right hand side is an old brick ice-house, relic of the days before electricity and refrigerators had reached this outpost. As the road to Easingwold crosses the main channel of the river – here the Ure – to Aldwark and Youlton, paradoxically it is Aldwark and not Ouseburn which has given its name to the river crossing – a toll bridge which has spanned the river for centuries- avoiding a 21-mile (34 km) diversion.

The present privately owned bridge, which dates from 1873 and replaces a structure built in 1772, is constructed of iron with long brick-arched approaches to allow flood water to pass beneath the single carriageway with its sleepered surface. When in 1772 Mr John Thompson first received from George III a charter to build a bridge to carry pack-animals and sheep instead of having to use a ferry, he was also granted as bridge-owner freedom from taxes, rates and estate duty – a right the owners still hold. After nearly two centuries the toll was doubled in 1980 to one penny for a pedestrian and 8 pence for a car but on 15 August 2005 it was increased to 40p on cars and £1 for trucks up to 7.5 tonnes – which is all the bridge can bear.

Walk across the bridge, which no longer offers access to the riverbank, and take the first road right at Bridge Farm; to your left is Aldwark Wood which was once part of the great Forest of Galtres. Continue down the road for just over half a mile (1km) until you approach Hunters Lodge on the right hand side. Just before Hunters Lodge is a path down to the river Ure. Take this path. → *page 19*

Aldwark toll bridge

The Ure rises in the mountainous region at Lady's Pillar between Yorkshire and Westmorland, collecting tributary streams as it glides through Wensleydale before being joined at Myton-on-Swale by the eponymous River Swale. This river derives its name from its swift course, having been called 'Swallow' by the Saxons and hence Swale. Many sources account for its existence which begins in the western extremity of North Yorkshire, described by William Camden as 'a dreary waste and silent wilderness'. From remote ages it has been looked upon as the 'holy river', for Paulinus is credited with having baptized many thousands of converts in this stream before churches, chapels and oratories were built. The Saxons held it sacred, and it was accounted by them as the Jordan of England from the fact that ten thousand are said to have been baptized in its waters in one day. The combination of these two rivers and a clutch of other streams uniting into one common channel results in a great volume of water. Consequently the soft, crumbly banks are always under attack and especially so when ravaged by the seasonal gouging of the swirling floodwaters and the debris they carry. But always they jostle beneath Aldwark toll-bridge for the supremacy which will be denied them within less than a mile by a leisurely paltry brook which will impose a new name-Ouse, a great absorber of other rivers and which itself will merge its waters before reaching the estuary and thus be denied both source and mouth in the popular sense.

Go through a gate and turn left over a stile onto the embankment and follow it beside the river to Linton Locks.

Along here are the stations of the patient fishermen whose devotion to their sport is akin to a religion. Numerous angling clubs lay claim to fish from various sections of the river bank, usually marked by gates which you will have to negotiate as you proceed forward betwixt one club and another.

After about a third of a mile (0.5 km) look to the other bank for Ouse Gill Beck. The little rivulet is no more than 3 feet (1 metre) wide at its mouth when it drifts into the indifferent main stream, changing its name from Ure to Ouse as if by some magic touch A small inscribed wooden signpost marks the spot.

Head south alongside the River Ouse which edges past rows of willow trees planted in recent times by the Yorkshire Water Authority. ↓

This was the western edge of the former royal Forest of Galtres, frequently mentioned in medieval records of York and according to contemporary descriptions particularly uninviting. 'Many places,' we are told 'were thick and shady with lofty trees and underwood but others were wet flat boggy moorish quagmires – a dreary waste extending north from York for twenty miles to Aldborough.' Galtres, we are told, means 'boars' brushwood' and it has been suggested that pigs raised on acorns in this once dense and diverse forest originally produced the meat for the distinctively flavoured York Ham. In 1215 King John ordered his bailiffs to 'allow the mayor and citizens of York to have what is necessary from the woods in your bailiwick for fortifying the same our city' and more timber was taken in the fourteenth century for buildings such as the Merchant Taylors and Merchant Adventurers Halls in York. Unfortunately the dense woodlands also provided shelter for thieves and vagabonds who preyed on unwary travellers passing through and for centuries the lantern burning in the tower of All Saints church at York was both a beacon of hope as well as of direction.

After a further 1½ miles (2km) you pass on your left Linton-on Ouse. There is a permissive footpath – until 2013 – from the river to Linton via Hall Garth which is the site of a former moated house. → *page* 21

Recorded in King William's Domesday Book of 1086 as 'Luitone' but big enough to have 1,440 acres of woodland and 20 acres of meadowland, the name has been spelled and interpreted variously down the years, but the 'Lin' part may well signify no more than 'by the water' (lake or river). On the other hand some people claim that the name is derived from the cultivation and processing there of 'line' or flax, of which there is some evidence.

The present status of Linton was determined by a Bachelor of Physick who bought the manor in February 1706. He was Doctor John Radcliffe, born in 1653 of wealthy parents in Wakefield and educated at the local grammar school as well as University College, Oxford. In 1682 he was practising in London and created a reputation for his fresh approach to the treatment of smallpox. He built up a rich clientele becoming physician to HRH the Princess Anne of Denmark, and for a generation was the most trusted consultant in London. He must have reaped rich rewards for he was to give Oxford the Radcliffe Camera and the Radcliffe Infirmary and, on his death in 1714, among many benefactions, bequeathed his estates at Linton to University College, entrusting them: 'to pay out yearly sufficient money to two medical students to complete their training over a period of ten years, half of which period must be spent abroad for their better improvement and so from time to time for ever. And, if any overplus of the said rents and profit of my Yorkshire Estate I will to be paid for ever to the University College in Oxon for the buying of perpetual advowsons for the members of the said College.' Administered by an agent as it has been for the past 260 years, much of the land is still held by University College, which also accounts for the presence of the College Arms' public house in the village.

However, the over-arching presence in Linton is undoubtedly the Royal Air Force Base, home of No. 1 Flying-Training School. The aerodrome started life as a bomber base in the mid 1930s, becoming operational on 13 May 1937. On the very first night of World War Two – in September 1939 – Whitley bombers flew from here to drop propaganda leaflets over Germany.

The base covers some 320 acres, virtually surrounded by the Ure, Ouse and Kyle so that aircraft taking off in any direction pass over one of these rivers. Consequently the station crest bears the motto A Flumine Impugnamus, meaning 'We strike over the river' – a motto which proved well founded when Whitley, Halifax and finally Lancaster bombers made raids from here over Europe- including the first thousand bomber raids on Cologne and Bremen – during the Second World War. After the war it was a base for fighter squadrons until 9 September 1957 when the flying-training school moved in.

To the North there is a vista of the great white horse cut in the turf of the plateau which stretches east from Roulston Scar along the Hambleton Hills. With an eye big enough for twenty people to sit in, the

Cruisers on River Ouse above Linton Lock

white horse is about 314 feet long and 228 feet high. A schoolmaster in Kilburn village, which sits 600 feet below the sheer rampart, is said to have created the giant in 1857 with the aid of another thirty men, and finance for the venture is believed to have come from an anonymous villager who made his fortune in London. A coat of about six tons of lime covers the giant, but restoration work is necessary from time to time if the Kilburn white horse is to stay white.

A little further along brings you to another monument – this time an entrepreneurial failure – which bestrides the river at Linton. ↓

John Smeaton's lock at Linton was all that resulted from the grandiose eighteenth-century up-river improvement schemes. And after a troublesome and tempestuous career it still remains there today as a quiet backwater providing peaceful surroundings for fishing, boating and caravanning.

See box on page 22

Walk past the back of Linton Lock Caravan/Camping Reception Block on the flood embankment. Cross the road leading to the lock and walk towards Linton Ings sluice gates, crossing these and then dropping down to the right to cross over the stile and back onto the river path to follow it towards Newton on Ouse with the church spire ahead. → page 23

Saga Of The Lock

From its inception the lock was destined for difficulties. In accordance with the 1770 Act of Parliament, the Linton Lock Company found itself supervised by a commission of 'thirty men of substance who were to have no financial interest, two of the members being the Lord Mayor of York and the Archbishop'. Once sworn in, they could neither resign nor sell their positions.

By 1852 it was being enthusiastically reported that 'the upper level of the River Ouse on which Linton is situate has of late undergone considerable improvement'. Local farmers were far from overjoyed, and frequent complaints were made about damage around the towpath, and of riverside meadows being under water.

Nevertheless the commissioners seem to have been capable and efficient administrators for in a three-month period in 1849 twenty-one vessels carried 1,717 tons of coal through the lock to Boroughbridge and forty-three more took 2,626 tons to Ripon; but during the whole of 1875 only 1,150 laden keels through. Despite the decline in traffic, Linton Lock Company became very prosperous, paying dividends until 1910 when the increase in rail traffic put an end to the days of high profits. In 1920 the remaining funds were embezzled by the clerk and treasurer, causing the company to collapse. The lock rapidly fell into disuse through lack of maintenance and virtually no income from tolls. Meanwhile, in 1923 Viscount Lascelles with HRH Princess Mary formally opened a small hydro-power-station built alongside the lock by York Corporation to supply the city and surrounding villages. Although it cost only £53,000, it became uneconomic with the installation sub-stations, and about 1963 it was closed.

The lock was badly damaged in 1947 by floods, which prompted a rescue operation by the Inland Waterways Association and Linton Lock Supporters Club who produced enough cash to repair and restore it for use a couple of years later. Sand-barges and pleasure-craft were the main users, but with tolls for commercial craft fixed at fourpence a ton by the Act of Establishment, the lock was uneconomic. In 1960 the bottom lock gates collapsed, and rescue operations started all over again, but in less than two years the lock was abandoned as the upper gates were also found to be liable to collapse. The demand for substantial expenditure on maintenance and debt-clearance seemed to herald the death-knell of the lock which was now becoming more and more neglected.

Salvation came in 1967 with the development of a marina with 70 pleasure-boat moorings on The Cut – a short canal stretch bypassing the weir – a caravan park and a café on a 25-acre site.

In 1982 tragedy struck once again when 300 boats were trapped above the lock by debris from January floods and contractors had to work 13-hour days removing about 10,000 tons of spoil and other obstructions.

Two years later an ambitious dredging program to clear The Cut was embarked on but in September 1986 the lock had to be closed again as repair costs of £100,000 could not be met. By October the commissioners had identified problems with the adjacent weir requiring a further £250,000 expenditure on repairs.

The Yorkshire Ouse and Ure Navigation Fund was set up and enough funds raised to provide a short-term holding operation so that the lock could operate once more in 1988 but by the beginning of 1999 erosion had accelerated and £60,000 was urgently needed to prevent the whole lock collapsing.

Local authorities agreed to make some contribution and British Waterways agreed to take over the lock once satisfactory repairs were completed. Work got under way in July 1990 and British Waterways subsequently took over responsibility.

The Ouse now makes a wide sweep and just before Newton the path veers off to the left to cross a ditch by means of a small brick arch and then on to steps up to a bridge crossing the River Kyle. ➜ *page 24*

This stream, though of little importance now, is supposed to have been navigable for flat bottomed boats during the time of the Romans and in 1815 the hulk of a vessel was discovered a few miles upstream. In the reign of Edward I the Kyle served as the boundary line of the Forest of Galtres. Although it assumes the title of river, the Kyle does not rise above the dignity of a beck. Nevertheless, this tributary and surrounding marsh land made boggy by seasonal flooding resulted in the erection of a bridge here many centuries ago. First mention of it comes in the Perambulation of the Forest of Galtres in 1316, 'following the Wall [that is the Wall of York] to the Water of Ouse, thence to Beningborough and Newton Bridge, and so by Linton Brook and the midst of Linton Marsh going on to the west of the village of Tollerton.'

Great debate and controversy at Quarter Sessions meetings of the North Riding magistrates centred on this bridge at the beginning of the seventeenth century. After being told it was in 'great decay' in 1606, the inhabitants of Linton in 1607 were indicted for not repairing 'the road from Aldwark to York'. They denied responsibility, claiming upkeep of the bridge was a county obligation, but their plea was overruled by the magistrates. Even so, little was done, and in 1608 the magistrates gave the villagers 'unto Midsummer next' to finish the task 'upon paine of £3 to everyone of the said inhabitants that makes default'. Whether this impelled everyone into a flurry of activity is not recorded

Continue along the path running parallel to the road, passing an open space at the back of a large house. This is Newton Landing. Where countless feet once trudged to and from waiting boats there is now nothing but a riot of marsh plants, for Newton Landing is under water at flood time, and the former rough-paved landing is now just a name for the tongue of land where the tiny River Kyle eases its waters into the Ouse. From Newton Landing follow the road and bear right into the village of Newton on Ouse.

2

Femmes Fatales
Newton on Ouse to Rawcliffe Ings

> **Start:** Cherry Tree Avenue, Newton on Ouse (Grid Ref 512600).
> **Distance:** Approx 6 miles/ 9.7 Kilometres.
> **Terrain:** Mainly river path.
> **Maps:** OS Landranger 100 & 105 Explorer 290.
> **Car Parking:** Cherry Tree Avenue.
> **Public Transport:** 29 Bus from York to Easingwold via Newton on Ouse (Stephenson's Coaches 01347 838990).
> **Refreshments:** Dawnay Arms and Blacksmith Arms, Newton on Ouse, Blacksmith Arms, Skelton, Riverside Farm Inn, Shipton Road

Entering Newton on Ouse from Newton Landing, turn right by the Green and walk along the cherry-tree lined avenue towards the church. (It is possible at Newton Landing to cross a bridge in the left hand corner behind the house and walk along the river behind the houses of the main street, through numerous gates

The Newton on Ouse Landing

and the odd stile to reach the path running around the perimeter of Beningbrough Hall). ➔ *page 27*

The tall white spire of All Saints' Church at Newton on Ouse overlooking the river is a landmark from as far distant as Brimham Rocks in Nidderdale and familiar to railway travellers between London and Scotland for over a century. In the middle of the nineteenth century the church was rebuilt except for its Norman tower, from which the graceful spire with flying buttresses rises to 150 feet. Equally dramatic is the big stone double-entrance lych-gate, not unlike an abbey gatehouse, with separate entrances for carriages and pedestrians.

A notice sternly warning visitors: 'There is no right of way to the river through the church' is a reminder that this sedate village haven was formerly a tourist magnet. Come here in the spring, when the glory of the cherry trees with pools of golden daffodils in a broad greensward is a sight to be remembered, or in the autumn it is framed by an arboreal mantle of red and gold, if you want to understand and appreciate its attraction.

Evidence of its appeal to York folk in the eighteenth-century can be found in old newspaper reports which solemnly testify: 'The City of

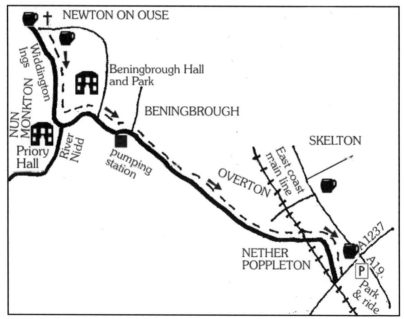

York steamer made four excursions to Newton on Ouse last Monday and Tuesday, and conveyed great numbers of passenger there and back ...' 'On Wednesday evening The Ariel' steamer sailed from Lendal Ferry on an excursion to Newton on Ouse and back with no less than between 500 and 600 persons on board. Walker's brass band accompanied the party, who reached York again, shortly after eleven o'clock without any other accident having been experienced except a man and a girl getting a complete immersion whilst attempting to get on board at starting ...' On Good Friday 21st April 1829, seven-year-old Cornelius Benton tried to jump from the packet-boat into a smaller one at Newton Landing and fell into the river. He was not rescued, for the York Courant of 19th May reported the finding of his body in the river near Ouse Bridge in York.

Cruisers at Nidd Mouth

The influx of visitors was always at its peak on the Tuesday and Wednesday of Whitsuntide during the nineteenth century when Newton Feast was held. Boat-loads of people came to enjoy on the village green and elsewhere what a local poet described as:

'Peddlers stalls with glittering toys displayed.
The various fairings of the country maid.'

The feast is still held annually and the Dawnay Arms inn still continues as it did then to dispense refreshment here.

Before continuing further you may care to join the other visitors who come here to marvel at the 375 acres of parkland with luxuriant woods and the gracious rooms of Beningborough Hall now restored and *administered by the National Trust in conjunction with the National Portrait Gallery.*

Continue past the church until you meet the gates of Beningbrough Hall. → page 29

Henry VIII granted the Beningbrough estate to John Banister in 1544, but it passed thereafter to his son-in-law's family, the Bourchiers, with whom it remained for the next two hundred years. John Bouchier who had inherited the family estates in 1700 at the age of 16, made a good marriage to a wealthy heiress which enabled him to pull down an Elizabethan house and in 1716 he hired York 'joyner and architect' William Thornton to build the present hall facing southwards over an expanse of parkland extending to the margin of the Ouse 'whose waters are often spotted with trading vessels'. At the time Thornton 'was look'd upon as the best artist in England' and consequently he created a showpiece of eighteenth century craftsmanship.

After the Bourchier line died out in 1827, Beningborough passed to the Dawnay family, until in 1917 it was sold. The tenth Earl and Countess of Chesterfield then made it home and brought there many of the historic contents of their ancestral seat, Holme Lacy in Herefordshire. The Treasury accepted the hall and park in part-payment of death-duties 1957 when the Countess died and it passed to the National Trust. A £400,000 restoration scheme was completed on 22 May 1979.

Beningbrough Hall, which has a wealth of extravagant baroque woodcarving and plaster, is home to a major exhibition from the National Portrait Gallery – over a hundred portraits of British celebrities from 1688 to 1760 on long-term loan. Besides fine works by Sir J Reynolds and Thomas Gainsborough, there are portraits of such notables as Pepys, Handel, Alexander Pope, Sir Robert Walpole and David Garrick.

This fine baroque house, some 130 feet long, and 60 feet wide is 70 feet high from cellar floor to chimneypots. The magnificent entrance hall rises through two floors to a height of 32 feet and a monumental staircase goes up to the salon on the first floor. Whilst upstairs elegant lords and extravagantly attired ladies enjoyed eighteenth century luxury surrounded by Baroque architecture, downstairs can be seen the mangles, flat irons, drying racks and other equipment in the more austere domain of housekeepers like Marian who had an ill-fated existence.

See box below

From Newton on Ouse the river heads directly south. To rejoin it, at Beningbrough park gates you bear right along a track signposted as a public footpath, passing a bungalow on your right to pass through a hand gate. Continue on the path at the edge of the field with some trees on your left to rejoin the river bank opposite Widdington Ings Head. Follow the well defined path downstream for about a mile (1½ km) along the beech-lined towpath of murderous repute as it skirts the Beningbrough estate past a water tower on your left to reach the confluence with the River Nidd at Nun Monkton on the opposite bank. ➜ *page* 31

Murder Most Foul

Explanation comes from a tale in the little book *Beningborough Hall* by James Leslie Armstrong of Wortley near Leeds which was printed in York but published in London in 1836. Forerunner perhaps of our modern docu-dramas beloved by television producers, it was advertised as an 'embellishment' of a happening that occurred in or about 1776.

The story concerns the wicked steward at the hall who contrived the dastardly murder of the virtuous housekeeper. The hall tenanted by Mr and Mrs Giles Earle – Mrs Earle having been formerly Margaret Bourchier – both of whom seem to have been abroad for much of their time. Political intrigue or persecution may have been the reason, but pecuniary embarrassment was probably more likely. Giles Earle's need for cash may well have induced him to offer for sale then 'a large quantity of valuable oak timber, proper for ship building, with some ash, elm, and sycamore trees', growing on or near the banks of the Ouse at Overton, Shipton, Beningborough and Newton. Ship-building timber was fetching up to three guineas a ton due to the demand for ships to build up a navy against the French who had joined the American rebels against Britain in the War of Independence. By happy chance the trees were conveniently sited near a main thoroughfare – the Ouse – which was provided with special 'landing-places' for shipping timber.

Against this background, housekeeper Marian was not surprised when two men arrived with instructions to pack all valuables into two boxes and await forwarding instructions. She arranged to store the boxes in the cottage of gamekeeper Martin Giles to whom she was engaged. Steward of the hall Philip Laurie discovered where the valuables were held and enlisted the help of a local layabout called William Vasey in a plan to steal them. Knowing that Marian, who had previously spurned his advances, took an evening stroll along a beech avenue, he waited for her behind a tree, pounced on the unsuspecting girl and threw the strangled body into the river.

Suicide was assumed at first, but imprints of boots in the mud and behind the tree suggested foul play. Paradoxically suspicion fell on her lover, doubtless due to his secretive manner over the preceding days when the valuables had been deposited with him. Taking advantage of this, Laurie and Vasey decided to steal the valuables and murder Martin. With Laurie keeping watch outside, Vasey broke into the cottage, but Martin awakened and managed to raise the alarm, which was answered by other servants – and Laurie. Vasey was captured and committed to York Castle, charged with burglary and attempted murder.

Word of the incident reached Mrs Earle, who travelled north. For some reason she suspected the involvement of Laurie and dismissed him with the news that Vasey was about to make a full confession. Laurie admitted his involvement but, finding no forgiveness, tried to shoot Mrs Earle and blew out his own brains. Vasey was tried and condemned and made a full confession before being hanged at the Tyburn on York Knavesmire on 18th August 1760. And the case was closed. Or was it? For soon afterwards a pale, neat figure with shoulders bowed and head bent clutching the remnants of a set of rosary beads was seen walking along the banks of the Ouse by many people. This tall, statuesque lady, who stooped as she walked, eventually disappeared in the churchyard of Newton on Ouse where the unfortunate Marian lay buried.

After a 55-mile journey which began on the slopes of Great Whernside the River Nidd now delivers its waters into a wide bend of the Ouse here, creating a sandy beach and a popular picnic spot for cruising enthusiasts.

Once linked by ferry to Beningbrough Hall, the village of Nun Monkton is where some God-fearing monks founded a settlement and built a monastery about eleven centuries ago. Alas, no ruin or trace remains to tell of its size and importance; yet in its former name of Monech-stone, the monk's town, there is sufficient evidence to reveal the story of its origin. What is more, the magnificent shrine which now stands on or near the site of the old monastery preserves the holy and devotional character of its original founders. Standing beside the broad waters of Ouse, the monastery must have been tempting bait for the pillaging Northmen of the ninth century, so not unexpectedly the building was ravaged, the monks slain or dispersed.

See box on page 31

Priory Hall, a handsome red-brick building in Queen Anne style, now stands on the site of the priory, overlooking the river but high

Merry Nuns Of Monkton

Shortly after the Conquest, Simon de Monckton was Lord of the Manor, and in the twelfth century William de Archer and his wife Ivetta founded a priory of Benedictine nuns in honour of the Blessed Virgin Mary, hence the present name of Nun Monkton. Unless tradition belies them, the fifteen nuns who lived here were not always as chaste as the sanctity of their vows would warrant. The priory was in the archdeaconry of Ripon, and at one time scandalous stories were whispered abroad about the then prioress Margaret Fairfax and the sweet guileless young things under her charge. Word of their 'carryings on' with one John Monkton and sundry kindred spirits resulted in a visitation in 1397 from Thomas de Dalby, Archdeacon of Ripon. He conducted a searching enquiry into the running of the priory. Margaret Fairfax was accused of wearing too fine linen, making too free with the funds and permitting her charges to wear 'precious furs, silken garments, rings of worth, tunics fastened with brooches after the manner of lay women' as well as attending divine service not properly attired. The natural desire occasionally to drop the cowl and scapular, to 'look nice', was perhaps a feminine trespass that would find many excusers, but there was the more serious imputation against the lady principal and her subordinates of undue intimacy with John Monkton and his amorous comrades, conduct which brought much scandal upon the house. The Archdeacon forbade them even to talk to males within their establishment, to stop accepting presents and to abandon the use of secular robes and jewellery. So ended the riverside trysts of John Monkton and his friends.

enough to be out of reach when the floods come – as they did in a memorable inundation of 1892 when the autumn waters were 22½ feet above normal. King George IV when Prince of Wales is said to have lunched here with the then owner, John Joliffe Tufnel, after attending York Races at Clifton Ings in 1789. Alongside the gardens is the old cobbled way down to the ferry landing where tourists once came from York on steamboat trips at a return fare of sixpence.

At the confluence of the Ouse and Nidd continue to follow the path as it skirts the Beningbrough estate. As you pass through a gate, continue forward a few metres up to the National Trust sign then bear right by a waymarker following the river as it flows south eastward towards the hamlet of Beningbrough. ➜ *page 32*

Peeping over the trees ahead of you is the distant spire of Shipton, setting for Act IV, Scene 1 of the second part of Shakespeare's King Henry IV. The formidable rebellion against the King in 1405 had Archbishop Scrope as one of its principal leaders. He preached a seditious sermon in York Minster, whereupon twenty thousand men joined his standard at York before marching out of the city through Bootham into the Forest of Galtres where they encamped near Shipton. The rebellion was a failure, and Scrope paid the penalty for his insurgence further downstream at Bishopthorpe.

Continue downstream and in about half a mile (0.75 km) you will arrive opposite the neat brick buildings with smoked-glass windows which mark the river intake, storage channel and pumping-station of the Yorkshire Water abstraction scheme. ↓

Designed to augment the water supplies of Leeds and, at times, other parts of South and West Yorkshire, it was built in 1978 at a cost of over £14,500,000 and pumps 15 million gallons of water a day through 28,600 metres of pipeline to a storage reservoir at Eccup, north of Leeds.

After about two more miles (3 km) through open farmland the path passes the little hamlet of Overton which was once the country residence of the abbots of York. ↓

The abbot of St Mary's Abbey alongside the river at York had the honour of being mitred and had a seat in Parliament, for which reason he enjoyed the title of Lord Abbot. Whenever he went from the abbey, his retinue was grand and numerous, so that his stately 5-mile journey up-river to Overton would have been colourful and spectacular. Alas, nothing remains now except parts of the moat, for the building was demolished in 1736 and some of its stones were incorporated into a farmhouse.

If you wish to cut short your walk, there is a turn off from the river to the A19, where you can catch a bus into York. Just past Overton, where the river bends eastward: take a signposted path on your left leading to a minor road where you bear right to go under the main railway line and after about three-quarters of a mile (1 km)you reach the A19 York-Teeside road opposite the *Blacksmiths Arms* at Skelton. Here you can catch a bus into York. Otherwise continue on along the river.

As if repulsed by the approaching municipality the river runs eastward as you follow the path and pass on the opposite bank the sprawling modernity of Nether Poppleton, which signals the arrival of suburbia. → *page 33*

Domesday Book of 1086 refers to Popletone (Nether) and it has sometimes been called Water Poppleton. The name was once believed to derive from an association with poppies as white poppies were a valuable crop grown for unripe seed capsules distilled to produce laudanum, a tincture of opium, which was supplied to St Leonard's Hospital in York.

The river continues making a broad sweep eastward and slicing across it overhead are the twin bridges carrying the main railway line linking London with Edinburgh and beyond, under which you pass. ✦

See box on page 34

From Nether Poppleton to York the Ouse flirts with the rail route whose shimmering rails run northwards to converge in infinity. Continue to follow the river path. It will meet the cycle path (Number 65) coming in from the left, so that the cycle path and footpath are united. Follow it for a short while until the cycle path bears to the left away from the river, just before a red bricked bungalow. You follow the river path to walk in front of the bungalow until it emerges from woodland and rejoins the cycle path.

If you are walking into York, cross the sluice gates ahead and walk on the flood protection embankment following the river. However, if you are intending to finish walking at Rawcliffe Ings, go along the cycle path and follow this to the outer ring road(A1237) or cross under the bridge and follow the footpath around until you meet on your left the footpath to the Rawcliffe Park & Ride. Whichever route you take, in front of you is the six-span bridge which carries the York outer bypass A1237 over the East Coast main line and the river. The £17 million outer ring road, on which work started in November 1984, was opened in sections during 1987 to provide a major link in the region's road network. The 10-mile(26 km) long highway involved construction of seven bridges, two across rivers, three over railways, and two other roads.

The Quest For Speed

The route was developed piecemeal, and until 1923 trains had to operate over the lines of three separate railway companies—the Great Northern, the North-Eastern and the North British—a situation which provoked the inevitable disputes. Indeed, as late as 1897 the North British suddenly terminated the agreement under which the main Anglo-Scottish expresses were worked through by North Eastern engines over North British metals, north of Berwick, until a dispute was settled. As a consequence the North British had to increase the running-speeds on its section of line in order to cover the time lost by changing engines at Berwick. Before the nineteenth century was over, rivalry on the railways was to produce some spectacular speed achievements on this route. The biggest outburst of competition was in the 'Railway Races to the North' between the East Coast and West Coast routes which took place on two occasions separated by a gap of seven years. The first 'round' was in 1888 and followed a decision to allow third-class passengers to use the 'Special Scotch Express' between London and Edinburgh. This train, the 10 a.m. from King's Cross, was to become in time the Flying Scotsman, and as running at beginning of 1888 it took nine hours for the 392.9 miles, although this schedule allowed time for a lunch stop. By the end of August when the races finished, the East Coast route had achieved an overall time of seven hours twenty-seven minutes in spite of the normal lunch stop at York and with, in addition, a delay at Selby while a hay-barge on the Ouse passed through the swing bridge there.

At the end of August 1888 the opposing railway companies got together and agreed not to indulge in further competition, but in July 1895 old rivalries flared up again when the West Coast companies—London and North Western and Caledonian—announced a cut of forty minutes off the timing of their overnight express to Aberdeen—a 523-mile run in 520 minutes. The East Coast response was immediate, but common sense prevailed after a derailment of a West Coast Scottish express at Preston, and so 'racing' ceased for several years. Gradually, due to a wide range of improvements over the years, the speeds have improved and continue to do so —dramatically.

3

Double Jeopardy

Rawcliffe Ings to Skeldergate Bridge

Start: Rawcliffe Ings can be accessed from A 1237 or from the Park & Ride at Rawcliffe Bar (Grid Ref 573546).
Distance: Approx 4 Miles/ 6 Kilometres.
Terrain: Level on river path and paved esplanade but some short flights of steps to access bridges.
Maps: Explorer 290; Landranger 105.
Car Parking: On slope alongside A1237, west of A19 roundabout into York and Park & Ride at Rawcliffe Bar.
Public Transport: Green Line 2 Bus services to Rawcliffe Park & Ride.
Refreshments: Numerous offering wide choice in York.

The first part of the route to Clifton Bridge follows the flood protection embankment. A quicker alternative would be to walk along the footpath/cycle route 65, which is to the east of the river.

If parked on the slope at the side of the A1237 to the east of the river then walk down the slope and walk straight ahead, over a stile and on to the flood protection embankment, then turn left. If you park at Rawcliffe Park & Ride, take the footpath to the City Centre and Beningborough, which is on the side of the Park & Ride away from the York Outer Ring Road. When you reach the footpath/cycle route running parallel with the Ings, turn right and follow it up to the bridge crossing the river. Just before you go under the bridge, cross the stile to go along the flood protection embankment, then turn left.

As you walk along the flood protection embankment, you move from Rawcliffe on to Clifton Ings. On the opposite bank are the Acomb Landing Waterworks, which once marked the city boundary, and extracts around 10 million gallons water a day to slake the thirsts of citizens and industry. ➔ *page 36*

In times of flood Clifton Ings holds back millions of cubic metres of floodwater to reduce the risk of inundations downstream, as well as providing some flood-protection to parts of Clifton and Rawcliffe. (See box on page 38) *In summer it is a kaleidoscope of colour from a profusion of wild flowers clustered in variegated bouquets wreathed in clumps of grasses, and casting off clouds of fragrance. A panoramic vista of the Minster in the distance comes into view as the flood protection embankment swings to the right in a big curve.*

See box on page 38

Were it otherwise, Clifton Ings would now be the Ascot of the north, for the earliest records of racing in Yorkshire date from 1633 and give this as the battleground, from 1709, on which the 4-mile heats were contested. Racing continued here until 1731, when the meeting had to be postponed due to the Ouse over-flowing and inundating the course. After this it was transferred to the Knavesmire on the other side of the city.

Nearer Clifton Bridge the flood protection embankment swings left, running parallel to the road and after crossing some sluice gates, it brings you back on to the footpath/cycle track (65) to take you under the bridge. ➔ *page 37*

The idea of building a bridge at Clifton had been discussed for more

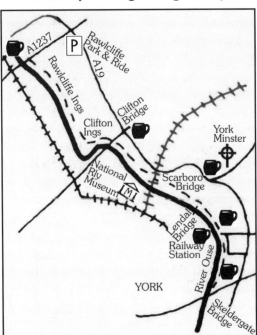

than fifty years, with plans, petitions, promises, talks and more plans, until the scheme earned the description of 'York's Comic Opera'. When proposed in 1913 the cost was estimated at £35,000.

Half a century later, on 28th October 1963, Lord Mayor Archibald Kirk opened the hotly-debated £230,000 six-span concrete bridge which links the two banks here with the observation that it was the first bridge to span the River Ouse since January 1881.

In Domesday Book *reference is made to the existence of Clifton in the time of Edward the Confessor. For centuries it formed part of the parish of St Olave's, never having a church of its own until the present structure built in 1867. Revered too was a tree reputed to be the last of the great Forest of Galtres. Standing by the roadside near Clifton Green, 300 metres north east of Clifton Bridge, it finally expired in the summer of 1948, and was unceremoniously removed.*

Pass under Clifton Bridge and continue along the riverside path into York city centre. ↓

The notorious Guy Fawkes inherited quite a lot of land hereabouts between Clifton and the river on which has stood St Peter's School since 1844 (on your left hand side at the first piece of open ground you come to) and where he is commemorated by a plaque on the schoolwalls.Originally founded by Paulinus in AD627 for the sons of thegns it was located at Horsefair, adjacent to modern Clarence Street, during the years when Guy Fawkes was a pupil. The great green sward of its 28 acres of playing-fields slopes gently down to the river.

As you approach the housing on the riverside, on the opposite bank is one of the magnets which make York an international tourist centre – the National Railway Museum housed in the former steam-engine shed which was a cathedral for railway-lovers. The exhibits range over every conceivable aspect of railways, large and small, old and new. The museum was formally opened by HRH the Duke of Edinburgh on 27th September 1975 – an especially appropriate choice in view of the royal rolling-stock preserved here. One exhibit with an unequalled power of attraction is Sir Nigel Gresley's famous 4-6-2 Class A4 locomotive Mallard No 4468 in its striking blue livery. On 3rd July 1938 Mallard reached 126 mph descending Stoke Bank to create a world-speed-record for steam locomotives.

Just past some 1930s housing, you reach Scarborough Bridge.→*page 39*

This crossing was built in 1844 to carry across the river the York to Scarborough railway from which it obviously derives its name. This was the first bridge within the city boundaries to share the labours of Ouse Bridge in providing facilities for foot-passengers to cross the river. Although primarily a railway bridge, it has always been supplemented by a footway for passengers. At first this was situated in the middle of the bridge between the up and down lines, but in 1874 a section about

In Memoriam

Summer serenity can soon turn to tragedy, as is evidenced by the only surviving grave in the shadow of the preserved seventeenth-century church tower of St Lawrence in York. On the afternoon of 19th August 1830 Fishergate nursery seedsman John Rigg's family of two daughters and four sons were full of high spirits, which doubtless prompted Mr Rigg to seek some activity to absorb their energies and give him a little peace. An outing on the river seemed a good idea, especially as they had a visitor − Miss Grace Robinson of Ayton near Scarborough − to entertain. Joined by Thomas Sellers, son of the Falcon Inn landlord, they set off upstream in a rowing-boat. The exuberant party met a keel coming down river under full sail when they were a hundred yards or so above Acomb, and whether there was a misunderstanding, an eddy in the river or an unexpected gust of wind we shall never know, but the pleasure-boat was struck by the speeding keel and the whole party flung into the river. Alas only two − Thomas Sellers and nine-year-old Jessy Rigg − survived. The shattering news was given to Mr Rigg when the bodies had been recovered, and a stunned public subscribed a monument to commemorate the calamity. Wild roses and briars strangle the stonework, and drifting leaves sometimes obscure the dedication, but beneath it lie nineteen-year-old Ann, seventeen-year-old Eliza, eighteen-year-old Thomas, sixteen-year-old John, seven-year-old James and six-year-old Charles. And to keep alive the circumstances of their demise Sheffield poet James Montgomery wrote a special epitaph:

> Mark the brief story of a summer's day!.
> At noon, youth, health, and beauty launched away;
> Ere eve, death wreck'd the bark, and quench'd their light,
> Their parents' home was desolate at night:.
> Each pass'd alone that gulf no one can see − .
> They met next moment in Eternity.
> riend, kinsman, stranger, dost thou not ask me where?.
> See God's right hand, and hope to find him there.

eight feet wide was built on the south side at a lower level than the railway portion, to take pedestrians across in a less alarming situation, as it does today.

Almost immediately on the left is Earlsborough Terrace which is a reminder that it was once the administrative centre of the province ruled by Tostig in the eleventh century. He was a tyrannous and bloodthirsty man who was a great raiser of tolls and taxes. Discontent with his rule came to a head in 1064. The insurrectionists rifled his mansion in the Earlsborough and drowned two hundred of his servants in the Ouse ' extra muros civitatis', − outside the walls of the city.

Go under the archway and turn back on yourself to cross the bridge. From the bridge you will have good views of the city skyline, particularly the church of All Saint's lantern tower in which once burned a brazier as a beacon for travellers approaching through the Forest of Galtres. Proceed along the opposite bank past the rowing club headquarters and the car park towards Lendal Bridge.
➜ *page 40*

On the left hand bank are the ten acres of Museum Gardens which provide a home for the ruins of St Mary's Abbey and the early-Victorian Greek-revival style building of the Yorkshire Museum. Built by the Yorkshire Philosophical Society to house its collection of antiques and geological specimens, it was formally opened by the then newly established British Association holding its first assembly here in September 1831.

Shortly afterwards the river front was piled and the esplanade constructed, being restored and paved in 1965 which is commemorated on an inscribed slab in the pavement. Flotillas of pleasure cruisers moor here in the summer.

Scarborough Railway Bridge

Pleasure Craft at Marygate Landing

St Mary's Abbey was founded in 1080 by Stephen of Lastingham and later enlarged by King William Rufus. It was suppressed in 1540 but most of the precinct walls built in the middle of the thirteenth century by Abbot Simon of Warwick still stand.

Also in the gardens alongside the river are the remains of the hospital of St Leonard whose riverside landing was down the narrow lane which you can now see on your the left. It is conjectured that Lendal arose from a slurred rendering of St Leonard's Lendynge Hill.

Ahead is Lendal Bridge where the city walls stop on either bank of the Ouse at which point there was for many years a ferry leased by the city Corporation to the highest bidder. → page 42

The creation of York's first railway station in Toft Green in 1840 made it necessary to have an additional road-crossing of the river, and the site of this ferry was the obvious choice. Disputes between the railway and city authorities on financing the project delayed progress, as did arguments about its design. Eventually in 1859 an Act of Parliament was obtained; construction began in 1860; and after a year of work the whole lot fell into the river, killing five men.

The present ornate structure by Thomas Page, engineer of Westminster Bridge and a gifted designer of iron structures, was

Lendal Bridge

opened for public use on 8th January 1863, replacing the ferry run by John Leeman since 1851. Four months later he was compensated for his loss of business with £15 together with a horse and cart. Tolls were charged and on the first day yielded £4. 5s 10d but the bridge became toll free on 7 August 1894,

Alongside the old ferry steps on your left is Barker Tower which served as a mortuary and a toll-bar in the fourteenth century. Chains are said to have been hung across the river here to prevent boats slipping away without paying dues and obstructing unwelcome visitors.

Abutting the eastern end of the bridge is St Leonard's Tower which was home to the former York Waterworks Company – one of the oldest water undertakings in the country – before it was acquired by Yorkshire Water. On 1st April 1677 a lease was granted by the Mayor and Commonalty to an enterprising London merchant called Henry Whistler' to erect and make a waterhouse and waterworks for the service and accomendac'on of the inhabitants of the said City of Yorke'. The lease provided for the laying of 'pipes, wheels and other engines and things necessary into the said river for the drawinge and conveyinge of water'. It was to run for five hundred years from 1677 at a rent 'of one Pepper Come on the feast day of All Saints in every yeare (if itt be lawfully demanded) and noe more'. In 2006 it was sold and developed as a luxury residential property.

Go forward through North Street Postern below Lendal Bridge and bear left into North Street. There has been a postern gate here for centuries but the present arch was built in 1840 to provide access to railway coal yards then just outside the walls. The original gateway was not wide enough to enable a horse and cart to pass through; only a horse. ↓

Known as Nordstreta in 1090, the origins of North Street are obscure but the gardens were presented to the city in 1959 as a perpetual open space.

On your right is the £15 million building constructed in 1991 from the same limestone used for the Minster, as a prestige headquarters for the General Accident Insurance Company which is now the Aviva home of Norwich Union.

Once in North Street, walk along for a few yards before turning left between two pillars into Joseph Rowntree Gardens, which border the riverside. ➜ page 43

Across the river is the Guildhall built in the fifteenth century on the site of a former Common Hall, where the original Roman ford crossed the river. The present building is a replica opened on 2 June 1960, for the original was largely destroyed by fire on 29 April 1942 by a wartime air raid of twenty German bombers. Inside are 120 carved bosses faithfully copied from photographs of the originals. Behind it is the Mansion House, official home of the Lord Mayor.

Further along on the right running parallel to All Saints Church is the narrow street called Tanner Row. This is more or less the line of the old Roman road to Tadcaster and it is thought that a ford here went across the river here to the fort.

The old building with the carved corner post is believed to be all that remains of a Dominican friary which stood here from 1228 to 1539. Alongside is All Saints Church with twelfth, thirteenth, fourteenth and fifteenth century architecture. In eleven windows is some of the finest medieval parish church glass. The six corporal acts of mercy according to the Gospel of St Matthew are shown in a window of c1410 and next to this is the fifteenth century Pricke of Conscience window, so called because it depicts the last fifteen days of the world as described in a medieval poem of the same name.

Continue to the end of the gardens and cross the little bridge to walk along a paved walkway along the riverside behind the hotel. ✚

In medieval times a narrow lane called 'Develynstanes' led from North Street to the river here. The name derives from Dyflinn the Scandinavian name for Dublin which was linked through York.

A plaque on the end wall is dedicated, 'To the memory of John Snow 1813-1858 Pioneer Anaesthetist and Epidemiologist. Born near here'. When ether and chloroform were introduced in 1846 and 1847 Dr Snow taught himself how to use them safely and gave over 4,000 chloroform anaesthetics without a death. Among his patients was Queen Victoria. He also identified the cause of a cholera outbreak in York was drinking water from the sewage infected river Ouse and he persuaded the city council to provide an alternative supply after which the outbreak cleared up.

The walkway exits on to Bridge Street at the corner of Ouse Bridge. A few yards to your right is a pedestrian crossing which you should use to cross this busy route before turning left to walk over the bridge. Walk down the first set of steps on the other side to take you down to King's Staith. ➜ page 44

The steps leading down to King's Staith have existed for many generations and for a time were called the Grecian Steps which was a corruption of the word Greces or Grees which simply meant steps. As early as the eleventh century there was some structure across the river here, possibly the wooden one which fell in 1154. Eighty years later Archbishop Walter de Grey granted a warrant authorising the building of a stone replacement. Consisting of six narrow arches on which stood shops, tenements, chantry chapel, and a gaol, the bridge, built in 1235, lasted three hundred years. Disaster overtook it in 1564 when a heavy snow fall and severe frost with a sudden thaw produced so much water and floating ice that the centre two arches collapsed and in the fall twelve houses were overthrown and twelve people drowned. This collection of buildings stood on the north side at the western end where it joined Bridge Street., which was originally Ouse Bridge End, probably because it was difficult to say where the bridge ended and the crowded buildings began. The Ouse Bridgemasters Rolls of 1435 lists 29 houses and shops on the south side and 23 on the north.

In 1566 the bridge and its buildings was restored over a period of fourteen years and it was in Ouse Bridge Hall that York Sunday School – thought to be the oldest in the country – was set up in 1786.

In the late eighteenth century the street was widened to become New Bridge Street, although the 'New' wore off at some point. A new bridge was begun on 10 December 1810 and completed in 1820. It was a toll bridge for the first nine years of its life, being made free on 18 June 1829.

See box on page 45

Across the river in 1660 Lord Mayor Christopher Topham promoted the construction of a small public wharf which for many years was known as Topham's Staith'. It was enlarged in 1678, but by the beginning of the nineteenth century was almost derelict so when the present Ouse Bridge was erected, a new wharf was constructed and given the name Queen's Staith to match its venerable counterpart.

This was only half its present length at first, but it was enlarged later and became the centre of the river coal-trade throughout the nineteenth century not surprisingly becoming known colloquially as 'Coal Staith'.

Walk forward past restaurants and along Friars Terrace and South Esplanade until you reach an open space before Skeldergate Bridge called St George's Field. ↓

A fragment of masonry on the riverside called Friar's Wall is a reminder of the magnificent Franciscan friary which was established along the riverside about 1250 and continued until the Suppression of 1539. It was these magnificent buildings in which a Parliament of Edward II met in 1322 and in which the Parliaments of Edward III assembled, where the King invariably resided during all his visits to York, and in which Richard II once stayed. Here, at the Tower Street end of the wall is a plaque bearing the official version of flood heights in the city.

Continue forward across St George's Field, so-named after the Templars Chapel of St George which once stood on this site. → page 46

From time immemorial this green space has belonged to the citizens with the right to 'walk, shoot with bow and arrow, and to dry linen'.

Across the river on a site which had been the centre of the city's river commerce in the Middle Ages, next to the Old Crane Wharf, is the bonding warehouse which originally opened for business on 26th May 1873. Skeldergate is said by some people to owe its existence to being the home of shield-makers. However others claim it is derived from an old dialect word 'upskill', meaning 'to unload' as when tipping a cart, and this seems more likely. Either way it was chosen as a location by Wilkie Collins for his book No Name, and Robinson Crusoe was born there in 1632 according to author Daniel Defoe.

Remains of St Mary's Abbey

Bridge Fever

Ouse Bridge has been the setting for some colourful occasions not least being a miracle attributed to the city's patron saint, St William, which is illustrated and immortalised in stained glass in one of the Minster transepts.

The occasion was the return from Rome of William Fitzherbert after he had been appointed Archbishop by the Pope in 1154. An excited populace turned out to greet him on the old wooden Ouse Bridge, but the multitude was so great that the bridge collapsed. Men, women, children, horses and dogs were thrown into the rolling flood in one tangled, shrieking mass. St William simply waved his crucifix over the seething tide, and lo and behold, it was like the parting of the Red Sea. They all walked out of the river as if it had been dry land, and not one was lost, not even so much as hurt, save one horse which suffered a broken leg Three weeks later the Archbishop developed a fever and died, and was buried in the nave of the Minster.

Immediately below Ouse Bridge the river finds itself constricted between two staiths – King's and Queen's. King's Staith, royal landing-point as its name implies, is lost in summer beneath a sea of tourists patronising the *Kings Arms Inn* and in winter submerged by the river.

Immediately ahead of you is Skeldergate Bridge. → page 47

The Corporation discussed Skeldergate Bridge for only five years before beginning to construct it. The foundation stone was laid on 12 June 1878, it was first used for pedestrians on 1 January 1881, and it was formally opened for general traffic on 10 March 1881. By then it had cost £56,000 – more than half as much again as the original estimate.

The little castellated toll-house is a reminder that for thirty-three years,

Official flood marker

Ornate lamp on Skeldergate Bridge

until 1st April 1914 when it was formally declared free of tolls, it cost a halfpenny to cross. The bridge was designed by Thomas Page – also responsible for Lendal Bridge – but he died before the council approved his plans and the job was taken over by George Gordon Page. Unlike Lendal Bridge the new bridge had to cope with tall-masted ships and was designed in three sections, a land arch over Skeldergate itself, a main arch over part of the river, and a small arch (under which you will pass) was moveable to allow navigation. By

1971 the lifting mechanism had seized up and a new fixed surface was laid over it.

To your left is a short flight of steps which you mount to access the bridge if you are leaving this section of the walk here.

Skeldergate Bridge

4

On Sacred Soil

Skeldergate Bridge to Naburn

Start: Skeldergate Bridge (Grid Ref 605514).
Distance: Approx 5 Miles/ 8.0 Kilometres.
Terrain: Level river path and quiet roads.
Maps: Explorer 290; Landranger 105.
Car Parking: St George's Field adjacent to Skeldergate Bridge.
Public Transport: 42 Arriva Bus Service York to Selby via Naburn.
Refreshments: Ebor Hotel, The Marcia Inn, and Woodman Inn, Bishopthorpe; Blacksmiths Arms,Naburn.

Go down to the east bank of the river from Skeldergate Bridge, heading towards its confluence with the River Foss. ➜ *page 52*

On your right across the river adjacent to the bridge is a multi-million pound development of 134 flats and luxury penthouses called Bishops Wharf, begun in 1988, on a site which was once a cherry or-

Bishops Wharf

The River Foss flood barrier

chard bought by Isaac Richardson, who came from a Quaker family of tanners in Whitby and set up a tannery here. He died in 1791 but his heirs by the mid-nineteenth century had developed a fertiliser works with adjacent wharf and were trading as Henry Richardson & Co. Fertiliser

production continued here until 1961.

Alongside the river is Terry Avenue which gained its name from a former Terry's Chocolate factory which also stood here.

In the early 1990s the avenue was restricted to pedestrians and cyclists along most of its length. It is now an important link in the York to Selby cycle path which is part of the 'White Rose Way' and the National Cycle Network.

Bisecting it is a street – Clementhorpe – where until the late 1920s a shipyard stood whose slipway into the river had to be crossed by a wooden footbridge. Complete with timber stores, sawpit, blacksmith shop, and paint and tar shop, office and so on, it was used to build barges for commercial operations. The Slip Inn further up the street perpetuates its memory.

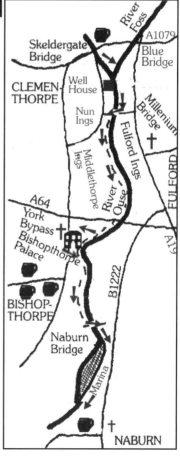

This whole area is known as Clementhorpe which some authorities claim means 'a small village colonised from a larger one' and this could allude to its location outside the city walls or the foundation of a breakaway religious house. The name was in use in 1070 long before St Clement's Priory was founded here by Archbishop Thurstan about 1130. He 'granted to God, St. Clement and the nuns of St Clement, the place on which their house was erected, together with two carucates (two carucates = twice as much land as a team of oxen could plough in a season) of land in the suburbs of York, and twenty shillings issuing from a fair in York'. The Priory from its foundation was an independent house, under the jurisdiction of no abbey, but subject only to the Archbishop of York, and when Archbishop Geoffrey in 1192 attempted to lower the status of the house Prioress Alicia went to Rome and made an appeal to the Pope. Though the Archbishop disregarded the appeal and excommunicated all the sisters, their cause eventually triumphed and the independence of the Nunnery was maintained.

The reputation of the nuns was not the most saintly and their hospitality was widely known; a privilege which seems to have been abused. On 24 March 1312 the abbot and monks of Selby were prohibited from visiting Clementhorpe or spending the night there, the social attractions evidently having been strongly in evidence to call forth this censure from the archbishop.

Isabel Warde was the last prioress and she was compelled to sell a silver chalice and cup to meet the extra expenses incurred when the

The Millennium Bridge

Commissioners of Henry VIII arrived at the Nunnery on 13 June 1536 for the Dissolution and disbanding of the community which was completed by 31 August.

Adjacent is Waterfront House – a residential refurbishment development completed in 1999 on a site which once served a very different purpose. Originally opened as a coal depot and wharf by the Equitable Industrial Society (forerunner of the Co-op) in 1899 it was later extended to house a bacon factory and bakery, supplying 482,096 loaves of bread and 1,161,056 pastries a year.

On your left across the car park is Castle Mills Lock built in 1794. Under an Act of 1793 the Foss Navigation Company had been given 'power and authority to purchase Lands, Tenements and Hereditaments... and to make and maintain a navigable communication for Boats, Barges and other Vessels ... from the Junction of the River Foss with the River Ouse ... to Stillington Mill'.

Also on your left across the Foss Basin is the rear of the £1.1 million Novotel officially opened on14 May 1988, and a modem housing development which stands on the site of the Anglo-Saxon city of Eoforwic – once the bustling hub of York's trade and industry.

Here in 1794 John Prince set up a glassworks but when he died in 1820 so did the business. It was revived in 1835 with the establishment

Fulford Hall across the River Ouse

of the York Flint and Glass Company by Joseph Spence and friends who produced decorative bottles bearing coats of arms, bee-hive glasses, drawer knobs in crystal, sapphire, jet, or canary yellow topaz. Despite these exotic creations the firm foundered in 1921 but nine years later the National Glass Company restarted the business which was modernised and successful enough to become a public company in October 1948 but once again it foundered and was closed in December 1983.

At the confluence of the two rivers at Blue Bridge, which derives its name from always being painted blue. ➜ *page 54*

Bishopthorpe Palace overlooking the River Ouse

A plan of 1736 shows a bridge here built after the corporation ordered 'Wardens of Walmgate to get such bridge as they thought proper made over Browney Dyke (the Foss as far as the lock) at the New Walk in St George's Close'. The Corporation paid £110.7s.0d for this simple blue-painted wooden drawbridge which was replaced in 1768 by a stone bridge with a wooden swivel section in the centre to allow the passage of masted vessels up the Foss.

Another replacement in 1834 gave way to an iron lifting bridge built in 1858. The current bridge, which dates from 1929-30. is the sixth on the site. The concrete emplacements on either side were to hold two cannons taken from the Great Redan at Sebastopol during the Crimean War and brought to York for the City's Crimean War Memorial on 5 November 1858 – the fourth anniversary of the Battle of Inkerman. Each gun was 8ft 3 ins long, weighed over 56 cwt and had fired 36lb shot. Alas the demands of Word War 2 saw them taken away to be melted down to make munitions.

To your left is Blue Bridge Lane. This formed the southern boundary of the grounds of St Andrew's Priory founded in 1202 for monks of the Order of St Gilbert of Sempringham.

In 1292 a royal licence was given to the prior to enclose a lane from Fishergate to 'the water of Use' but the canons seem to have been less fortunate than other orders in obtaining revenues and the priory fell on hard times. Although the grounds covered about six acres the monastery never figured much in city life and when it was 'axed' in 1539 there was only a prior and three monks.

From its source at Pond Head or Oulson Reservoir about a mile west of Yearsley north of the city, the River Foss follows a tortuous 24-mile course before joining the Ouse here.

With a catchment area of 125 square kilometres the river discharges into the River Ouse where the lower reaches originally formed a moat augmenting the formal defences along the eastern boundary of the city. The £4 million flood alleviation scheme here was officially opened on 28 February 1989 by John MacGregor, Minister of Agriculture, to protect nearly 600 homes affected by serious flooding in 1982. The scheme includes an 8 metres wide by 7.5 metres high steel turnover lift gate weighing 16 tonnes, which is closed when the Ouse rises 2.8 metres above normal level, and a pumping station with eight pumps *that discharge flood water from the Foss downstream at a rate of 1,800 tonnes a minute.*

Cross the bridge and continue forward into New Walk, keeping to the left hand side of the path, as there is a bicycle lane on the right hand side. ➜ *page 55*

Sparkling ladies of Georgian York and their attendant beaux had high social ambitions, so in 1731 a forward-looking Corporation hit on the idea of a promenade along the Ouse. Two years later, trees were planted and a broad, gravelled walk was laid out on the riverside length of St George's Fields, at the expense of the city.

According to Hargrove the nineteenth century historian, 'The branches of the trees, having been trained over the walk, form an interesting avenue of luxuriant foliage which is not only rural and extremely pleasant but in summer screens the rays of the sun and hence is a favourite resort for the citizens.'

The original scheme provided for a parade the length of St George's Fields, but the Corporation liked its handiwork so much that in 1739 it took advantage of the little wooden Blue Bridge to extended New Walk south towards Fulford. The Corporation also decided to make New Walk into a really spacious promenade by increasing the width from 8 to 28 feet.

At the turn off to Hartoft Street at the junction with Lastingham Terrace you will pass a curious structure which houses a spring of water called Pikeing Well – later known both as Lady Well and Spring Well.

'A remarkably fine spring of clear water' was how local historian William Hargrove described it in 1818. 'The door,' he said, 'is frequently opened by a man appointed to take care of it; the water is drunk by many persons, and is also much used as an eye-water. An open receiver in front of the Well House is visited every morning for these purposes when the well is not open'.

Several wells existed along this stretch of the river and as far back as 1749 the Corporation had agreed to 'contract with proper workmen for the making of an hansom fountain at Pikeing Well'. But it was not built until 1756 when York's famous architect John Carr got the job to design it as an imitation stone ruin. Although he died in 1807 worth £150,000 after having designed such masterpieces as Harewood House he did not get the agreed price for his more humble commission, as the York Chamberlain's account book of 16th May 1757 testifies:

'Paid to Mr John Carr for erecting the building about Pikeing Well, he having allowed £25 for his freedom, £63.13s'.

In 1858 a re-building of this well house was carried out by Thomas Pickersgill the City Surveyor. The structure, which is now listed grade II was restored in 2000 as part of the Millennium Bridge project. From here you can see ahead the graceful structure of the Millennium Bridge crossing the river.

▌ Continue along the riverbank. ✦

Notice on the opposite side the very attractive gates that mark the entrance to Rowntree Park which was given to the city by Rowntree & Co Ltd at the close of the Great War (1914-18). The gates are in memory of all those from the Rowntree factory (then known as the Cocoa Works) who lost their lives in the Second World War (1939-45).

Just before you reach the 160 metre Millennium Bridge notice on your right two short sections of narrow gauge railway track to the river edge whose purpose is explained across the bridge where a stone plinth is inscribed: 'The Millennium Bridge is the first permanent bridge on this site. A temporary bailey bridge was erected in July 1955 during the York Tattoo. For over a century, a ferry service operated upstream of the bridge site, from New Walk to Clementhorpe. Military stores were unloaded at an Ordnance Wharf, built in 1888 and taken to the army depot in Hospital Fields Road on a narrow gauge railway, a small section of is still visible at the southern end of New Walk. Explosives were brought in the schooner 'Princess' known locally as the 'Powder boat'. In 1996 a competition amongst local school children considered possible methods for a crossing at this point and the inspiration for the Millennium Bridge was conceived'.

Designed for cyclists and pedestrians and built at a cost of £4.2 m the crossing was officially opened by HRH the Duke of York on 29 May 2001.

▌ Cross the bridge and turn left to walk along the river path. As the metalled path turns right, keep going straight ahead and cross over a stile into Nun Ings to follow a grassy path along the river to Bishopthorpe. ➜ *page 56*

Alongside the opposite bank are about thirty moorings of what twenty-five enthusiasts founded in 1933 as the York Motor Boat Club, becoming York Motor Yacht Club in the 1960s. In 1954 the club acquired a former First World War prison hospital building in Cumbria, brought it to York and adapted it as the clubhouse which is still in use.

Just before the river starts to make a broad bend to the right on the opposite bank is Fulford Ings, setting for the Battle of Fulford in 1066 when Earl Tostig, bent on recovering his lost earldom and supported by the forces of Harald Hardrada, King of Norway, clashed with the men of Jorvik led by Morcar, Earl of Northumberland and his brother Edwin, Earl of Mercia.

The Norwegians won and ravished York but only five days later, on 25 September, retribution followed with a resounding defeat at the Battle of Stamford Bridge. The survivors could man only twenty-four of the 315 ships that had brought the invading army up the River Ouse to Riccall.

Much of the fighting took place in a ditch called Germany Beck which runs into the river here. This strange name is thought to originate from the time when a certain German de Brettgate had a toft and croft in Fulford (1258-1270). About 1616 a bold plan was put forward to build a gigantic tidal canal of about 25 miles in almost direct line from Germany Beck to Blacktoft on the Humber which, had it succeeded, would have considerably shorted our walk. As always, finance was scarce, and it never came to fruition

Further along opposite Fulford Hall, the river swings west across Middlethorpe Ings. Scourge of the towpath at this point is the ghoulish apparition which on dark nights, to the terror and dismay of observers, appears as a headless lady clothed in white. Apparently many years ago a lady had been strolling by the river one summer evening when some miscreant jumped from a clump of tress and strangled her to death. Bent on pursuing her murderer, she started to come forth at the witching hour, wandering to and fro in the vain hope that she would find her attacker and bring him to justice. Headless but wrapped in a winding-sheet, she is said to be less offensive to local inhabitants than strangers, and when wearied with her fruitless errand, she returns to her dusty bed.

Go under the twin concrete viaducts which carry the A64 outer by-pass road over the river. ➔ *page 57*

The £750,000 five-span concrete bridge is the largest of eighteen bridges on the 14-kilometre bypass which cost £9 million and was officially opened on 14ᵗʰ April 1976.

Follow the path until it meets on the right hand side the fenced boundary of the crematorium and then on the left the fenced gardens of Bishopthorpe Palace, home of the Archbishop of York. The fenced path will lead you out through a gate on to Bishopthorpe Road, where you turn left along the narrow pavement to follow the boundary fence of the Palace Gardens. ↓

The title of Archbishop has been held since AD735 when Egbert, cousin of King Coelwulf received the official appointment from Rome.

On your right is the parish church of St Andrew built in fifteenth-century style between 1888-1903 by Hodgson Fowler.

National history is enshrined in a stained glass window given in 1951 in memory of Harrison Woodward's family. One panel shows Archbishop Drummond's church from 1765 to 1842 and the other shows it after Archbishop Harcourt had refaced the west end in stone in 1842. The bottom panel shows a dramatic scene of a tragic event in our history; Archbishop Scrope, manacled, with two other nobles, also manacled, being condemned to death in the presence of King Henry IV.

Carved in the oak roof above are the correct armorial shields of seven famous Archbishops of York who have lived at Bishopthorpe Palace and worshipped in the village church – Walter de Grey, Henry Drummond, Markham, Harcourt, Musgrave, Thomson and McLagan.

Having skirted on your left the tree-shrouded palace grounds, alive with squirrels and many species of birds, you arrive at the fanciful gatehouse. → *page 58*

Adorned with battlements, pinnacles, gargoyles and pyramid canopy, it was built almost entirely of stone from the ruins of Cawood Castle by Archbishop Drummond in the middle of the eighteenth century. The blue-faced six-foot-wide clock in the tower was salvaged from a former- stable block and is inscribed 'T.H. 1744' which is believed to refer to Archbishop Herring.

The site was bought in 1226 by Archbishop Walter de Grey for his palace, and the Manor of Thorpe St Andrew took on a new role and a new name. Here in 1405 Archbishop Richard Scrope, described as 'learned, charitable, devout, humble-minded, courteous and affable to all' stood trial in the great hall for rebelling against Henry IV, and when Chief Justice Gascoigne refused to pass sentence, the King ordered a local lawyer called Fulthorpe to pronounce judgement.

At one time passing sailors would fire a salute and be rewarded by the Archbishop with flagons of ale, but Archbishop Musgrave stopped the custom and thereafter the bargees always seemed to find it necessary to emit quantities of black smoke as they passed Bishopthorpe.

See box on page 59

Glance to your right up the village Main Street which boasts three curious pubs. First on the left is the Ebor Inn *which was originally* The Brown Cow, *but nobody seems to know why the name was changed. In 1884 the inn was sold by Tadcaster Tower Brewery as The Ebor and the inventory, which listed eight rooms including a dairy and a brew house, also included in the sale iron and wooden spittoons and the form with a stuffed seat On the right is* The Marcia *public house. Marcia, alias Spiderbrusher, was a famous racehorse bred by the late William Fenwick. In 1776 the horse won 125 guineas and a hogshead of claret from Sir Laurence Dundas's* Pontac *at York and went on to win other races at Lincoln and Morpeth. In 1777 she became the property of William Garforth who named her* Marcia *for whom she also won several races before she died in the spring of 1779. Almost opposite on the left is* The Woodman *with a large colourful tiled sign put up when it was modernised between the wars.*

Where the main road bends right into the Main Street, you turn left into Chantry Lane which takes you past Ramsey House on your right and through a gateway back to the river bank. ➜ *page 59*

Named after the previous Archbishop of York, who had just been enthroned as the 100th Archbishop of Canterbury in 1961, the house was built for Mr Arthur Gladwin. He was a Methodist preacher for more than sixty years and a former joint general manager of the Yorkshire Life Assurance Company. He died aged 88 in February 1983. Past it is an excellent view of the palace back garden and ahead is the ruined old village church of St Andrew's, built of red brick in 1768 by Archbishop Drummond on the site of a much older stone church which dated back to 1215. In 1842 Archbishop Harcourt restored it but the River Ouse gradually eroded the foundations and it was largely pulled down in 1899.

The beautiful west front still stands proudly enriched with leafy niches, pinnacles and buttresses with faces and finials, whilst a bellcote crowns its gable. On the site of the altar Archbishop McLagan put up a tall cross and on this is written: 'On this spot there stood for centuries the Parish Church of St Andrew, Bishopthorpe. Rebuilt on another site

AD1899'. Archbishop Drummond and his two grand-daughters are buried under the cross. In 1892 the churchyard was almost entirely under water and the site was abandoned in favour of a new one behind the palace.

Bear right a short way along the river bank to reach on the right a cottage beside Ferry Lane. ➔ *page 60*

Beating the Bounds

Bishopthorpe Palace had close links with St Martins, Micklegate and a curious incident happened in 1307 when Archbishop Greenfield had to issue a licence for officials to sprinkle holy water in the churchyard of St Martins, which had been polluted – two boys were fighting in it, and the nose of one of them had bled!

Another link with that parish and a youthful custom which must have entertained or puzzled river travellers in bygone days is recalled by a worn stone, part buried in the sand immediately opposite the palace. Despite the ravages of wind, rain and flood, the inscription clearly reads. 'Boundary St Martin's, Micklegate'. Although that was the essentially utilitarian purpose for which it was erected, it also served a principal function on the Beating of the Bounds, an event which took place every Ascension Day, attended by incidents whose superstitious origins are lost in the mists of antiquity.

After rambling round the parishes of St Martin's and St Gregory's at Fulford the vicar, church-wardens, parish clerk sextons, choir and parishioners assembled at the porch of St Martin's where they were fortified with bread and ale before setting out equipped with wands and ladders. At various points there were boundary stones or iron plates, and each was visited in turn before what was known as 'The Long Perambulation' took place.

Everyone walked by the riverside, carrying wands, a pitcher and a cock which had usually been bought in York Market. When the crowd arrived at Water Fulford Hall, as many as possible squeezed into the porch where there was a boundary stone, over which the pitcher was broken. Some people have suggested that this curious ceremony may have some connection with the old superstition of breaking pottery on Good Friday, as the points of the broken pieces were thought to pierce the body of Judas. Another practice at Water Fulford was to set a chalk-mark on the post of the chimney in the kitchen or hall, and this seems likely to have been a relic of the more permanent witch-marks which were a protective feature of North Riding cottage fireplaces. Sometimes the owner of the hall gave the visitors something to eat, but it is unlikely that John Key did when he lived there between 1803 and 1812. Mr Key was convinced he was paying too high a church rate – £18 in 1812 – and thought some of this money was going towards payment for the customary Bounds-beaters' dinner. In an old Estate

Book he writes: 'They had so much dining and drinking I sent Jasper Smith to complain. They came in two coaches, a shameful imposition!'

From Water Fulford the beaters rambled beside the sluggish waters until they reached the boundary obelisk opposite the Archbishop's Palace. Here on this stone any new-comer was bumped or bounced three times. The sexton who carried a bundle of willows under his arm 'picked the willows' upon various parcels of land before the assembly made its way across the fields to another inscribed stone in the hedge separating Buttery Bush Field from Matthew Close. On the way to this stone the cock was liberated, and all the boys gave chase, the one who caught it being acknowledged as owner before it was beheaded on the stone. After the ritual execution of the cock, the perambulating parishioners returned to St Martin's, before dining at one of the nearby inns. In 1850 the whole ceremony lapsed.

In 1899 the parish council decided that all material being off-loaded at the ferry landing here and not intended for use in the village should be charged three pence a ton. Also, if goods remained on the landing for more than a fortnight, five shillings was to be charged. The objective of this substantial penalty was less to raise revenue and more to keep the landing clear for Mr J. Sanderson who was paying one shilling a year for the privilege of using his ferry-boat.

Continue past the slipway and go straight ahead for just over two thirds of a mile (1 km) to reach the former railway swing bridge which used to carry the East Coast main line before it was diverted in 1983 to protect the Selby coalfield. This is now a walking and cycling route decorated with a four-metre high steel sculpture – The Fisher of Dreams – depicting an angler with a rod in his hand and a dog at his side. Whilst it is possible to continue on the opposite bank to Acaster Malbis for about a mile (1.5 km) there is no longer a ferry service and so it is not possible to re-cross the river. Bear to the right before the bridge, along a metalled path until you reach a path rising to your left to take you on to the former railway and across the bridge. Once across the bridge walk along for another 280 yards (250 metres) then descending to the left to turn right along the B1222 to walk into Naburn, passing the Marina on the right.

This vast marina was excavated on an 18-acre site and later extended to provide anchorage for over 500 vessels .It was opened on 17 July 1970. Take the first turning right into Front Street, where the slipway down to the river is a reminder of former ferry links.

Sources of Sadness

Naburn to Cawood

Unfortunately, this section involves mostly road walking as there are no paths either along or close to the river. Whilst there is a path on the opposite bank the confluence of the River Wharfe with the Ouse near Cawood has no crossing point and so precludes use of that path. However, the village of Stillingfleet is

Cawood Bridge

the jewel of this section and makes up for the deficiencies of the route. Take extra care when walking the road section. The B1222 from Naburn to Cawood is not a busy route but drivers tend to travel quite fast. There are verges to the road (in some sections open fields) for the majority of the walk. During late spring and summer the grass on the verges can be quite high, though they are cut from time to time.

Walk to the end of Front Street in Naburn bear left and then turn right to join York Road B1222 and continue along the road for about half a mile (1 km) to the driveway on your right down to Naburn Lock with its unique monument of the canal era. ➜ *page 64*

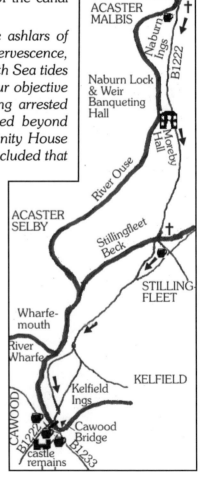

Here the river cascades over the ashlars of Naburn weir in a sheet of white effervescence, before greeting the waters of the North Sea tides and it could be reasonably argued our objective has been accomplished. Before being arrested here, these surging waters penetrated beyond York, and when two brethren of Trinity House examined the river in 1698, they concluded that big tides flowed to 'popleton fferry wch is about 4 miles above ye Citty (of York) & we could not learn yt except upon extraordinary Tides it ever flowed Higher'. Prior to 1757 all vessels bound for York had to reach the city with the tide, which did not flow more than 4 feet at Ouse Bridge, with the consequence that only vessels of very small tonnage could penetrate that far – a fact that entrepreneurial merchants viewed with chagrin. York Corporation took up the vexed question, vigorously petitioning Parliament until legislation was passed enabling them to make various improvements to the river. In particular, they were able to

Naburn Weir, marking the tidal limit of the River Ouse

build a lock at Naburn – at a cost of £10,000. Opened in 1757 with a toll of 14 pence levied on every vessel passing through, the lock was hailed as a great stride towards boosting river navigation for commerce to York. With up to 150 tons of cargo, vessels could now reach the heart of the city, and for considerably more than a century it usefully served the purpose for which it was built. However, it became increasingly obvious that the capacity of the lock – 90 feet long, 21 feet wide and 10 feet 6 inches deep – was insufficient for direct sea-going trade because most merchandise had to be trans shipped at Hull or Goole, incurring a loss of time and the imposition of dock dues. In an effort to overcome this severe handicap, it was proposed to enlarge the meagre dimensions, but the resultant disruption was considered too risky and costly. The solution was to construct a new lock alongside the old one and dredge various parts of the river. In particular it was necessary to be rid of a huge shoal of gravels and clays, well over a mile long, which had become an unwelcome feature near Acaster Selby. In addition to heavy deposits of silt, the shoal had built up from tons of earth as sections of the soft banks had slipped into the stream when the current was too weak to bear away the debris. Stubbornly defying the most strenuous efforts at removal, as well as breaking the hearts of keel-masters and labourers alike during the eighteenth century, the shoal had grown to more than two miles (3 km) in length by 1834, when it was eventually removed at considerable cost.

The new lock at Naburn was formally opened, amidst great rejoicing, by Prince Albert Victor, on 22nd July 1888, when all vessels carrying 200 tons or more were allowed to pass through free of tolls all day. The Wild Rose *carrying a cargo of 720 quarters of wheat – the largest consignment that had ever passed up to York until then – was the first vessel to be piloted through the lock. Less fortunate was the Goole steamship* Her Majesty *which, due to one of those inevitable ironies of fate which are an embarrassing feature of all such ceremonies, could not be manoeuvred into the new lock, despite having a beam supposedly a foot narrower than the chamber. Nevertheless the 152-foot-long and 26-foot-wide lock, which is 13 feet 6 inches deep, is capable of accommodating vessels with up to 400 tonnes of cargo.*

See box on page 65

Retrace your steps back up the lane to rejoin the B1222 which skirts the eastern boundary of Moreby Hall and its estate – as does the river on the west. Turn right and walk along the road for about 4km (2.5 miles) to Stillingfleet whose tiny beck waters the Ouse. ➜ *page 65*

On your left is the church of St Helena with is great oaken door on which is symbolic ironwork representing Adam and Eve, the Ark and the Trinity.

Some authorities claim that the boat figure symbolises not the Ark but the ravaging Danish fleet which is said to have moored in the Ouse around the mouth of Stillingfleet Beck. Could this event be responsible for the 'Stivelingflet' – the 'fleet of Stiveling – from which Stillingfleet originates?

Every available place in and around the church was occupied by over two thousand mourners for the interment of victims claimed by the river in a horrific Christmas tragedy nearly two centuries ago. Commemorating the event are two large stones in the graveyard near the road, on one of which is inscribed:

'Those whose names are here recorded were accidentally drowned in the River Ouse whilst returning from singing the praises of their Saviour in the neighbouring townships on December 26th 1833.

God's Will Be Done.

As a tribute of respect to the memory of the sufferers and of deep compassion for their sorrowing families, their common landlord, Bielby Thompson of Escrick Park has erected this monument.'

At the opposite end the headstone records the names of eleven victims who were aged between fourteen and fifty-six.

See box on page 68

Continue forward and cross Stillingfleet Beck by the hump-backed stone bridge on the central parapet of which is an iron plaque as a perpetual reminder that the Ouse sometimes comes visiting. The

Scandal and Sleaze

Perhaps the most novel and surprising feature of Naburn Lock is the presence of a Banqueting Hall (the only one of its type in the country purpose-built as a function hall) which caused a scandal lasting over a decade when it was built and was almost certainly outside statutory powers of the river trustees who were labelled by a government commission as inefficient, lethargic and corrupt.

In the early 1800's the Ouse Navigation Trustees were effectively a committee of York City Council and part of a municipal administration. They had paid little attention to looking after the river and making money from tolls (by 1835 they had debts of £16,000 and an annual income of just over £2000) while building themselves this large and infrequently used banqueting hall in 1823-4. The stern Yorkshire Gazette said that this cost was 'the most indefensible part of their conduct'.

Historian William Camidge, writing after the fuss had died down much later in the century, said that the hall had been built to hold 85-90 people for dinner, and was equipped with large kitchens to match. It was, he said, 'not quite out of the way of the floods'.

The hall had been planned for the site of the former lock house at a cost of £1200 and was finished for over twice the amount, the trustees hastily blaming the architect for producing a building better than the one they envisaged. 'Very long and very angry contentions arose out of the addition of this room to the building necessary for the lock-keeper ...' which was 'engendering a good deal of refreshing at the expense of the river dues'.

For the then extravagant sum of £2742 the trustees received what was recently described as 'an impressive example of a late classical style with some characteristics of the Greek revival, particularly in its massive scale, the orderly and regular arrangements of the windows and the unusual details of its porch'. For good measure the floor of the main hall is cambered which experts concluded was a deliberate design to copy the deck of a vessel. Since it was built it has been used for official banquets on only two recorded occasions the principal one being the entertainment of His Royal Highness Prince Albert Victor of Wales at the official opening of Naburn Lock on 27 July 1888.

The hall became increasingly dilapidated and in 1976 York City Council estimated the cost of restoration at £75,000 so they applied for permission to demolish the building but the Environment Department ruled it was of historic interest as a monument of the canal age and should be preserved.

In 1982, York City Council acting on behalf of the Ouse and Foss Navigation Trustees sold the Grade Two listed building, together with about 30 acres of land, for £500. It was then converted into a hotel-restaurant but the first winter it was opened the hall was marooned by floods. Three years later the business was wound up and it re-opened as the Naburn Lock Hotel in 1989. Once again in 2008 it is being offered for sale.

inscription reads: ' This tablet was erected by grateful parishioners to commemorate the great flood of March 22nd to 29th 1947. Also in memory of the kindness shown by Capt. Boyle for the loan of a boat and Mr A Elcock and his crew. Depth of water 21 feet.'

Turn right now to walk along the southern side of the green. Continue to the end past Swallow House with its timber-framed upper storey which may be seventeenth century or earlier, on to the grassy area. In its south west corner is a gate, which will bring you into a field. Walk up the side of the field, where a gate leads you back out on to the B1222. Turn right and for your next turn off follow the road for about 1.3 miles (2 km). Look out first for Kelfield Grange on the left and then about 500 metres further on, where the road bends left, take a marked footpath on your right back on to the flood protection barrier of the River Ouse. Follow this and in just

The carollers' gravestone

under 1km, (half a mile) you will come to Wharfe`s Mouth.
→ *page 67*

The River Wharfe rises some two and a half miles above Outershaw high up on the bleak moorland expanse of Cam Fell in Langstrothdale in the Craven District of the Pennines some 1,273 feet above sea level. Here the headwaters of the river start their 69-mile(111km) journey to the Ouse. Some claim it takes its name from a Saxon word 'guerf'' which means 'swift', whilst others say it is derived from the Old English weopan

Stillingfleet church and the carollers' gravestone

meaning 'to throw' or 'to twist', later being associated with the Scandinavian hverfr, for 'winding'. The river drains one-twentieth of the area of Yorkshire and supplies the majority of the water for Leeds.

Follow the bend of the river on the flood protection barrier to a fine gateway at the top of a flight of steps giving access on to Cawood Bridge.
→ *page 70*

Nearby is said to be an ancient paved ford over the Ouse which can sometimes be located at low water and giving rise to yet another claim that Dick Turpin on his mare 'Black Bess' crossed here when making his famous dash from London to York after relieving unsuspecting travellers of their wealth. Clearly most people prefer to make a drier crossing, and a ferry once did brisk business, but in 1872 local businessmen replaced it with the substantial but narrow 295-foot iron bridge which is still giving service. A few yards, albeit at a maximum speed of 10 miles an hour, and you have crossed from one bank to the other, painlessly and with ease. But it was not always so. One night in November 1869, before the bridge was built, the carrier's wagon from York to Cawood was being ferried across in the then customary way. Storm clouds hung low, and the wind was howling across the open fields, catching the tarpaulins of the covered wagon and causing the

Christmas Carollers Tragedy

Filled with seasonal goodwill, the village choir had been in their places on Christmas morning to give the traditional service added zest with an enthusiastic rendition of popular carols and hymns. Boxing Day was a Thursday, and fourteen of them gathered in the village street at half past one ready to continue the annual custom of visiting Moreby, Acaster Selby and Kelfield, to sing carols at the principal farmhouses in and around these villages. After visiting a house at Moreby near the river, the carollers embarked in John Turner's boat for the river crossing at Low Acaster. After more hymns they embarked once again, a little after four o'clock, to re-cross the river at Stillingfleet which necessitated sailing down-river about half a mile. By now it was dusk as John Fisher and George Eccles rowed the little vessel which was being carried along by a swift ebb current running at the rate of five miles an hour. About a quarter of a mile from Acaster Selby they met a coal-laden barge called Perseverance being hauled upstream with a horse driven by Stephen Green. Both Eccles and Fisher intended to keep on the Stillingfleet side of the barge, but Turner told them to row to the other side. As he was a fisherman and they were agricultural labourers, they assumed he knew best and duly complied.

What happened next seems a little unclear. Apparently Turner shouted to the hauler to slacken his tow-rope, but Green thought he was being asked to tighten it. Doubtless the cries were distorted and blown back by the wind, and as the two vessels closed, the occupants of the little boat tried to avoid the line, but it caught the stern, capsized the boat and pitched everyone into the swirling river. In the melee that followed, the barge ran aground, but in the confusion, the screams, the struggles, the battle for life and the darkness, nothing could be done to rescue the unfortunate carollers. Fisher, Eccles and Richard Toes were rescued, but after two days of dragging the river only nine other bodies were recovered – Sarah Spencer, aged sixteen and Sarah Eccles, aged seventeen, leaving no trace except a shawl. A coroner's inquest at the *White Swan Inn* and a searching investigation were held, but the only outcome was the fine of one shilling on the moving cause of the accident – the boat.

Thirty parishioners dug the grave, measuring 21 ft by 7ft where the unfortunate victims were brought in threes to be interred by the stunned villagers.

Two days after the interment the *York Courant* headed a lengthy report of the 'Shocking Event' with a three-verse hymn to remind readers that 'God moves in mysterious ways, His wonders to perform'.

ferryboat to be unmanageable. Blown down the river, it collided with a barge, upsetting wagon and people into the river. One boatman in a tiny dinghy came to the rescue of two people, the driver and his wife, Bessie, struggling in the icy water. Leaning over the side, the boatman grabbed them both, but, finding himself unequal to the task, he gasped, 'Ah can only save yan, which 'es it to be?' 'Save Bessie,' was the virtuous answer of the drowning carrier as he slid from the grasp of the boatman into the Stygian waters of the river, never to be seen again. His was the only life lost, and Bessie Pilmer lived many a long year to relate the tale of her magnanimous spouse.

The gatehouse of Cawood Castle

Following this disaster a public meeting was held on 17th January 1870 at which it was arranged to raise £5,500 by the issue of shares and £2,700 by donations from landowners and others to build a bridge. York Corporation as river conservators agreed to contribute £150, and so the first pile was driven on 8th November 1870, the formal opening taking place on 31st July 1872 and the citizens had got themselves a 295 ft iron swing bridge. The Corporation found reasons for not paying the promised £150, and Alderman Francis Carr, who was Sheriff of the city and had also chaired the public meeting, was so outraged at their calumny that he resigned, paying a penalty of £50 to the city whilst donating £150 to the bridge funds and £100 to various charities.

Entering the river near the bridge is the Bishop Dyke (turn first left into Old Road and stand on the wall of flood protection barrier to see this) which runs down from Sherburn-in-Elmet and is said to have been known and used by the Romans. More than six hundred years ago the Dean and Chapter of York took in a quarry in the area on a lease for eighty years, followed by another period of nine-teen years. Tradition has it that the course of this stream was straightened, widened and deepened, so that stone from Huddlestone quarry might be floated down on rafts to Cawood for transhipment to boats going up-river to York.

Cross the bridge and walk up High Street to the traffic lights where you turn left on Thorpe Lane which carries the B1223. After about a hundred yards you will see on your right the Landmark Trust lodgings which now embraces the gatehouse ruins of Cawood Castle – setting for the 'Humpty Dumpty' nursery rhyme.

See box below

Little remains of the great castle, apart from this fifteenth-century gatehouse with two oriels and a vaulted archway. The 'Humpty Dumpty' rhyme is believed to be an allusion to the fall of the great churchman Cardinal Wolsey. To the castle here came the 'old man broken with the storms of State' who had neglected his Cawood home when busily in favour at Court, but after his banishment he tried to make amends – so much so that he employed three hundred craftsmen on repair work, and with his penance he is said to have spent the happiest period of his life

---

Humpty Dumpty Slept Here.

Of all these doings my lord knew nothing, for they stopped the stairs so no man could pass up again that was come down. At the last one of my lord's servants chanced to look down into the hall, and returned to my lord and showed him that my Lord of Northumberland was in the hall; whereat my lord marvelled, and would not believe him at the first. 'Then (quoth my lord) I am sorry that we have dined; notwithstanding he shall have such as we have with a right good will and loving heart. We will go down and meet him, and bring him up.'

With that he put the table from him and rose up. Going down, he encountered the earl upon the midst of the stairs, coming up with all his men about him. As soon as my lord espied the earl he put off his cap and said to him, 'My Lord, ye be most heartily welcome,' and therewith they embraced each other.

'Although, my lord (quoth he), that I have often desired and wish in my heart to see you in my house, yet if ye had loved me as I do you ye would have sent me word before of your coming, that I might have received you according to your honour and mine. Notwithstanding, ye shall have such cheer as I am able to make with you, with a right good will, trusting that ye will accept the same of me as of your very old and loving friend'.

This said, he took the earl by the hand and led him to his bed-chamber, and they, being there all alone (save only I that kept the door), these two lords standing at a window by the chimney, the earl trembling said, with a very faint and soft voice unto my lord, laying his hand upon his arm, 'My lord, I arrest you of high treason'. With which words my lord was marvellously astonished, standing still a long space without further words.

The next morning my lord rose up, supposing that he should have departed that day; howbeit he was kept close secretly in his chamber, expecting continually his departure from thence. Then I resorted to my lord, but as soon as he perceived me coming in he fell into such a woeful lamentation with such rueful terms and watery eyes, that it would have caused the flintiest heart to have relented and burst for sorrow. We comforted him, but it would not be. I sat him down to dinner, with whom sat divers of the earl's gentlemen; notwithstanding my lord did eat very little meat but would many times burst out suddenly in tears, with the most sorrowful words that hath been heard of any woeful creature. And I suppose there was not a dry eye among all the gentlemen sitting at the table with him.

The next day, being Sunday, my lord prepared himself to ride when he should be commanded. It drew fast to night. There was assigned to attend upon him five of us, his own servants and no more, and when he should go down the stairs out of the great chamber my lord demanded for the rest of his servants. They came to him in the great chamber and there kneeled down before him, among whom was not one dry eye. To whom my lord gave comfortable words and worthy praises for their diligent faithfulness and honest truth towards him, assuring them that what chances so ever should happen unto him he was a true man and just to his sovereign lord. And thus, with a lamentable manner, shaking each by the hands, was fain to depart, the night drew so fast upon them.

My lord's mule and our horses were ready brought into the inner court, where we mounted and, coming to the gate, the porter opened the same to let us pass, where was ready attending a great number of gentlemen with their servants, such as the earl assigned to conduct and attend upon his person that night to Pomfret (Pontefract). The number of people of the country that were assembled at the gates which lamented his departure was wondrous, about the number of 3,000 persons, who, after they had a sight of his person, cried all with a loud voice, 'God, save your Grace! The foul evil take all them that hath thus taken you from us!' Thus they ran crying after him through the town of Cawood, they loved him so well.

here. He professed himself a convert from ambition, and we are told that 'having suffered the perils of shipwreck he was thankful that at last he had cast anchor in a calm and pleasant haven, with the expectation of safety and rest'. His expectations were both short-lived and unfulfilled, for two days before his long-overdue installation as Archbishop of York he had an unexpected visit from the Earl of Northumberland and a posse of attendants. What happened next is best told by a man who was there – George Cavendish. His Life of Woolsey, *written in 1557, graphically portrays the drama of his master's fall.*

Naburn Marina

6

Devoted Duo

Cawood Bridge to Selby Bridge

Start: Cawood Bridge on B1222 (Grid Ref 575378).
Distance: Approx 8 Miles/13 Kilometres.
Terrain: Riverside path and quiet roads.
Maps: Explorer 290; Landranger 105.
Car Parking: Car park in Old Road next to bridge (Access via Thorpe Lane).
Public Transport: 42 Arriva Service from York to Selby via Cawood.
Refreshments: The Ferry Inn, Jolly Sailor and Castle Inn, Cawood, Grey Horse, Kelfield and several places in Selby.

The walk is on the east side of the river but before you start the walk, it is worth taking a look at All Saints Parish Church, Cawood. To do this, from the bridge take the first left into Old Road, which leads to a paved pathway in front of attractive cottages, including some dating from the late eighteenth and early nineteenth century, overlooking the river. This takes you to the church which is a conspicuous riverside landmark. ↓

Inside is a monument to a seventeenth century Archbishop of York, George Montaign This son of a local Cawood farmer rose to become the head of the church in the North of England. Sadly, after the day of his enthronement, he died during the night. Thus 'He was scarcely warm in his seat than he was cold in his coffin.' He was an apt punster with a ready wit. When the See of York became vacant, the king was at a loss for some time to name a fit person for that sacred office, and requested Bishop Montaign's opinion on the subject. He replied· 'Hads't thou faith as a grain of mustard seed, thou would'st say to this mountain' (at the same time laying his hand upon his chest) 'be thou removed into that See'.

After visiting the church retrace your steps to the bridge, cross over it with care and turn right at a gate, immediately after the crossing on to the flood protection embankment. This route will take you to the tiny slumbering village of Kelfield. You enter it over a stile just past a beacon with a sign that the village was formerly called 'Chelchefelt' in the domesday Book, 1086. ↓

See box on page 75

Walk along the main street of the village, bearing left with it until you come to a road on the right signposted to Riccall. Take the Riccall road. Walk along it for about two-thirds of a mile (1 km) until you reach a settlement of houses. Just before a row of cottages on the right, take a metalled track, cross a parking area and, keeping to the field edge, go straight ahead through a gate. Take care as this path is rather overgrown but at the end of the enclosed area it brings you out to an open space with a pond on the left hand side. Turn left, keeping the pond to your left; pass the back of a nursing home and cross another stile on to the river embankment. You can see Riccall to your left as the river bends south and just past Wheel Hall Farm is a tiny beck, emptying its waters into the Ouse and at which point began a great tragedy – the invasion of Yorkshire. → *page 76*

Harald Hardrada, the renowned King of Norway, moored in this quiet backwater his five hundred ships which had borne a vast army of Norsemen from the wilds of Scandinavia and the Orkneys for the conquest of England. Disembarking here, they marched through Ricall to attack York, triumphed over the Saxon army of defenders who barred their progress at Fulford and by nightfall on Wednesday 20 September 1066 were flying over the city the infamous banner of the land-ravager.

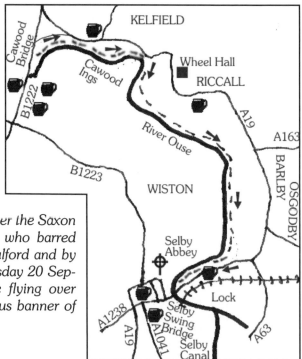

Follies Of Infatuation

How different the scene early in the nineteenth century when Kelfield was invaded by thousands of people in what must have been like the combination of a rock festival and a Billy Graham crusade. The event had its origins in Beedhams Court, which was an enclave of squalid lodging houses off Skeldergate and close to Queen's Staith in York. The area was known graphically as Hagworm's Nest, notorious for prostitution and disease, having the dubious accolade as the source of cholera in 1551, 1604 and 1832. Resident in, and possibly owners of the court were the Beedham family, a female member of which joined a religious community early in life, having become deeply religious. Here she found an opportunity to preach, and, professing great sanctity, she soon became popular with many followers, helped no doubt by the novelty of being a female preacher. She was in great demand, although she did have some peculiar religious notions, amongst which was the fervent assertion that she had been in a trance and walked with God, who had revealed to her the exact day and month she would die. Just how dramatic the impact of Hannah's preaching must have been is evidenced by reports in the *York Courant* and even *The Times* of Thursday 18 July 1833 reprinted an account from the *Yorkshire Gazette*. From then on she rarely preached without announcing this impending event, and as the time approached, she bid farewell to her family and friends, having for some unknown reason selected little Kelfield as the hallowed spot where the weary wheels of her life would cease to turn.

Whilst awaiting the appointed time -9 pm – she was royally entertained by one of her firmest disciples – a respectable farmer and gardener named James Sturdy. On the specified day – Thursday 1st August 1833 – thousands of people from towns and villages, far and near, journeyed by foot, horseback, cart and wagon, to be present at the spectacle. According to the *York Courant* 'places distant as Ferrybridge, Leeds and Doncaster swelled this spring-tide of fanaticism. On Wednesday night, the city bellman announced the departure from this city, next forenoon, of a vessel for the land of wonders, which would take out passengers and bring them back at a shilling a head. Great numbers availed themselves of this conveyance'.

Meanwhile Hannah lay in a snow-white bed holding court for the visitors as an unending queue of a thousand or more passed by her and hundreds more noisily speculated on the probabilities of her dying on schedule. Apart from Kelfield every village nearby was crowded, and within a radius of three miles there was a complete traffic-jam with conveyances of every size and shape full of people straining their ears for tidings of her life and death. When the appointed moment came, the excitement was at fever pitch, but despite her lips being frequently moistened with wine she could not die, and there were too many onlookers to permit suicide. The Methodist Chapel was opened and numerous people assembled there to pray – processions singing funeral hymns passed along the village street, and as one observer put it 'the scene was one of the most extraordinary that has been witnessed in modern times'.

The wearied and disappointed thousands who for many months previously had discussed this much-publicized event lingered after midnight, eagerly digesting each new piece of gossip and rumour. Then, chagrined and angry, they returned with a message of disappointment to other waiting crowds who had remained in neighbouring towns and villages for tidings. A great band of followers from York had gone on their curious errand, and crowds stood half the night awaiting their reports of the issues of life and death. The services of the Town Crier were called upon to relay the news at midnight and not unnaturally the cynical press took a 'we told you so' attitude to what they had already dubbed the 'nine days' wonder.' Only an overwhelming body of testimonials convinced the crowds that their fond dream had not been realized and persuaded them to go home as morning dawned.

Not everyone was disappointed. The event had provided the ferryman at Cawood with an unexpected bonus of £13 from transporting visitors across the river and out of gratitude he offered to give Hannah free passage and his wife generously presented her with a new gown. No evidence has been produced to suggest Hannah was attempting to exploit public gullibility.

She subsequently married William White on 29 December 1835, produced two daughters, died (for real) on 23 December 1839, and was buried in an unmarked grave at Holy Trinity church, Goodramgate, York.

Their triumph was brief. On learning that King Harold was advancing to the rescue, the Norsemen retreated to a position on the River Derwent at Stamford Bridge, where on 25th September 1066 they did fierce and bloody battle with Harold's Saxon followers. Thousands perished, including Harald Hardrada, and the remnants of the invading Norse army fled across country from Stamford to Riccall. The Saxon Chronicle records that: 'The English from behind smote them until they came to their ships, some were drowned and others were burned, so that few were left to carry back to Norway the dismal story.' Magnanimous in victory, Harold graciously allowed the survivors to escape on condition that they would be peaceful in future, but, of the five hundred vessels bearing the mighty host of warriors who had proudly entered the Humber a few days previously, only twenty-four ships were needed to take back the survivors.

Continue along the river embankment. Walk up to a gate on the flood protection scheme and turn right to skirt the back of industrial buildings some of which are occupied by the Environment Agency.

After about 100 yards (90 metres) go left over a stile and on to the flood protection embankment again. It is along this section that you will get your first sighting of Selby Abbey through the trees, though you have to wait until the river bends around by Barlby before you get the best views. It is also here that you get one of the few views looking along the river as opposed to looking across it. Before the big bend in the river the flood protection embankment veers to the left towards sewage works. ↓

Plaque marking the former pinfold in Kelfield

On the opposite side of the river is the little village of Wistow which gave its name to a coal mine.

Cross the stile straight ahead, turn right and go around the edge of a field, following the path up to the farm. Keep the farm buildings on your left and follow the path along the river, crossing a little footbridge taking you to the concrete and brick wall, protecting Barlby from the river.

For ease of walking, just walk a few metres left to the start of the wall and walk on the side of the barrier away from the river.

You keep to this route by the river all the way to the Selby Swing Bridge – a former toll bridge. You pass the Barlby Road which serves the industrial environs of Selby where a number of agricultural mills and other industrial premises are located. As you enter Selby you

The Grey Horse and Main Street, Kelfield

will see The Quay on your right with the dominating Ideal Flour Mill beside it. The path narrows to go behind two small houses and finally brings you out at the swing bridge.

If you wish to visit the Abbey, cross the bridge, go straight ahead along The Crescent, which will bring you to the Abbey entrance

Although the first toll to cross the river on a bridge here was probably imposed in 1794, the origins of the levy go back to the time of William the Conqueror rampaging around the North in the 1060s to put down regional rebellion against his Norman invasion. While he stopped off in Saxon Selby, his queen gave birth to a son who became Henry 1. William founded Selby Abbey in celebration of the birth. The religious house attracted nuns who were later given the right to run a ferry across the Ouse from what is now Church Hill, Selby, and charge a fee.

Selby Abbey

Selby Market Cross, adjacent to the Abbey

When Henry VIII did away with the nunneries the service passed into private hands.

By 1790 the ferry was very much behind the times since a survey showed that 11,795 people, 3,052 of them on horseback, used the ferry every month, so the owner, Baron Petre of Writtle, asked Parliament for permission to build a bridge; the museum preserves a model of the old trestle bridge which was taken to Westminster for Parliament to show what Selby wanted.

Even before the first bridge was built in 1792, battle raged between powerful factions for and against the structure, depending on their particular vested privilege. Local landowners and traders who promoted the bridge were opposed by the Ouse Navigation authorities who saw it as a threat to the river trade and their income, despite it having a 31 ft clearance which could be opened and closed within a minute. They were supported by Lord Lovaine, Earl of Beverley, who derived income from three down-river ferries. Eventually a panel of independent mediators was set up, and on 18th November 1791 they announced: 'We do unanimously award, adjudge, declare, and determine that according to the present existing circumstances only, a bridge at Selby will be a great and daily benefit to the public'.

The battle was won – temporarily at least. The Selby Bridge Act of 1791 empowered a company of twenty five individuals known as proprietors to construct and operate the bridge, provided for finance and tolls, laid down compensation for the ferry-owners and safeguarded the rights of the Ouse navigation authorities. Baron Petre was included as a proprietor but was to receive £25 annual compensation for his loss of ferry rights.

Winstanley, a leading engineer of the day started construction of the wooden bridge in 1792 and in August the following year John Tomlinson was hired as toll collector and swing bridge operator for £36 a year.

Fairly elaborate provisions for protecting the interests of shipping ensured that, amongst other things, vessels were always to be given preference over other traffic. The engineers eschewed the bascule principle of opening a span, so typical of the eighteenth century, and so Selby Bridge is one of the oldest with a swinging span. A novel feature of the mechanism was the early use of ball-bearings on a large scale which helped to open the cumbersome structure in less than a minute. Frequent collisions by coasters over the years with the massive wooden piers resulted in the structure being rebuilt with steel stays in 1969-70.

In 1892 and 1900 local authorities started talks to buy out the shareholders but their efforts came to nothing. The two-stage rise in tolls to 7p for vehicles and 6p a tonne for lorries in the 1980s brought renewed demands for abolition of tolls and Selby District Council even petitioned the Queen in 1988. Tolls were eventually removed on Thursday 19 September 1989 and in 1990 with government support North Yorkshire Council borrowed £500,00 to add to funds raised locally and the bridge was acquired in May 1991.

Thus the 'bridge of sighs', as the notorious toll-bridge was called locally, one of the severest bottlenecks of its kind in the north of England, cursed alike by coaster captains navigating to Selby and frustrated truck drivers with destinations on the opposite bank, was finally freed on Thursday 19 September 1991 when a coach and horses paid the last vehicular toll and a local schoolboy the last pedestrian levy.

For half a century Selby toll bridge enjoyed its solo position across the Ouse here, but between 1838 and 1840 the Hull and Selby Railway Company was extending its metal tentacles and needed a crossing. Since this would be the first rail-crossing of the river, the river authorities were not over-enthusiastic, but with precedence promised for river traffic they relented, and on 1st July 1840 a cast-iron bascule structure – the twin bascules lifting at the centre of a 45-foot-wide channel – was opened alongside for rail traffic. On 1st February 1891 it was replaced by the present unpretentious cast-iron swing bridge.

See box on page 81

Amongst the many treasures of Selby Abbey is a fourteenth century stained glass window, the design of which is thought to have been the model for the Stars and Stripes, donated by the English ancestors of George Washington, the first president of the United States. It shows the coat of arms of his forbears, the de Wessyngtons, which depicts three spiked spur wheels above the two red bars across a white shield. Washington is known to have used the heraldic device on two of his personal seals and a bookplate.

Wessyngton, which had various spellings until it evolved into Washington, comes from the Anglo Saxon Hwas, a Saxon chief's name, inga, meaning 'family of', and tun, an estate. Historians believe the coat of arms was probably included in the window to commemorate John Wessington, a medieval Prior of Durham. He also decorated the battlements of the tower with a frieze of washing tubs or tuns, a rebus – or visual pun – on his name.

Mind Of A Monk

The Benedictine monk, himself named Benedict, had sailed from France and, having passed up the Humber, was now in the less turbulent waters of the Ouse. Suddenly three swans alighted on the water, so he too landed, planting his cross upon the site which is today marked by Selby's magnificent old abbey and immortalised in their coat of arms.

Apparently our eleventh-century hero was a sweet, guileless old bald-pate with a light-fingered knack of finding and appropriating things that belonged to his brother monks at Auxerre. In his simple, childlike innocence he would discover their loose change and annexe their supper beer and would doubtless have stolen the bald spots on the brothers' crowns if they had not been attached. The mystic suddenness with which various properties had vanished prompted Benedict's brethren to seek a solution in their gentle monkish fashion. But the wily Benedict forestalled them by revealing that he had seen a vision in which the patron saint of the monastery appeared. And the vision advised him to leave for pastures new, so he hastily packed his spare vestments and prepared to depart the monastery. Less charitable writers might suggest he had an ear to the ground or an eye to a keyhole. However the magpie-feeling was still strong within him, and before leaving he succumbed to his instincts and acquired the most treasured relic of the convent – the finger of the patron saint, St Germanus. What he wanted with this portion of another gentleman's anatomy that was not convertible property is hard to contemplate. Perhaps he wanted to guzzle the liquor in which it was preserved. So it came to pass that this godly and simple-minded old freebooter, after being tossed about on land and sea, eventually sailed up the Ouse and came to rest at Seal Bay, Seil-by or Selby, a 'bay much frequented by seals'. Doubtless they were really porpoises but no matter our hero decided it was the place for him and promptly set up house under an oak tree. His household furniture was basic in the extreme – a wooden cross and the purloined finger of St Germanus.

Benedict has left us a fine word-picture of the sylvan scene as it appealed to his mind on his first coming. With the freshness of the landscape before him he describes it; 'A most pleasant place, covered as well with frequent groves as crowned with an ample tidal river like an earthly paradise.(and only ten miles from York). The intervening windings of the river are covered on every side with woods and groves, which provide much beauty in a pleasant place; among these many big groves, excellent in quality, properly lie near and belong to this domain. In the profits of the water this vicinity furnishes much, the lakes, and dams abounding in fishes'.

Its charm in the vista, he adds, includes his own home.' In the meantime, a monastery, as fair as notable, sits in its revered mass...The tower of the Church far off from those walking can be seen from every part, and with the roofs of the offices arising beside it as in steps, appear and are pointed out; and also, whatever is brought to York by ships from parts beyond the seas, or carried away from it to other parts of England, is wont to pass before the gates of the monastery of Selby'.

When he was not out poaching either game or fish, we are told, he spent much time in devotion, until one day William the Conqueror himself happened to call, intent on paying his respects to the devoted monastic burglar – doubtless they had much in common. As a result of his reception, the Norman conqueror bestowed rich lands for the endowment of that sacred edifice, the Abbey Church of Selby. Not unexpectedly, the enterprising Benedict, who had forsaken Auxerre as a refuge, assumed the role of first abbot, whilst continuing to annexe trifles as before. This is, of course, an outrageous version of the legend, but it probably goes much nearer the absolute truth whilst retaining the kernel of tradition

Joined by others intent on building a suitable noble structure, Benedict and his monks were faced with the problem of getting stone from the Fryston district some 8 or 9 miles distant. The solution they conceived was to improve a beck, known as Selby Dam, and for over a century the task of floating stone on rafts continued as each generation of monks pursued the arduous and painstaking task of building their house of prayer. At the confluence of the beck with the Ouse there appears to have been an anchorage, and it is tempting to suggest that this was the original 'seal bay'.

7

Fallacies Exposed

Selby to Hemingbrough

Start: Former toll bridge over River Ouse, Selby (Grid Ref 617326).
Distance: 6 miles/ 9.7Kilometres.
Terrain: Flood Protection Scheme.
Maps: Explorer 290; Landranger 105.
Car Parking: Car parks in Selby.
Public Transport: Bus services 415 York to Selby and 4 between
Selby and Howden via Hemingbrough. Rail Services to Selby
from Leeds, York and Hull.
Refreshments: Numerous and varied in Selby; The Crown, Fox
& Pheasant in Hemingbrough, also bakery and village store.

R eturning from Selby town centre recross the toll bridge to the eastern bank – this is one of the oldest timber bridges surviving anywhere in the country – and turn right to go under the railway line carried over the river by its swing bridge and along Ouse Bank, with its row of cottages well below river level. ➜ *page 88*

Selby's formerly grandiose buildings along Ousegate, looking out over disused remnants of wharves and jetties, are a reminder that by 1698 the little market town had carved a supreme position for itself as the 'place upon ye Ouse to wch most goods either imported from

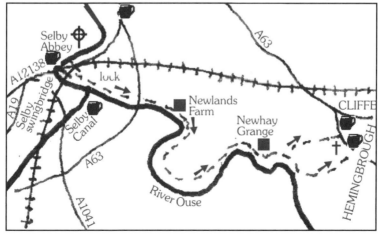

Hemingbrough Church spire

abroade or to be Exported and thither are now brought'. Just how extensive the trade was can be gathered from a description by the mariners and watermen who claimed they possessed 'several vessels of good burthern which are constantly employed in carrying great quantities of woollen manufactures, lead, butter, corn rape-seed, tallow and several other commodities, to Hull, London, Newcastle and several parts beyond the seas, from whence they bring all sorts of merchandise

Small Link in Big Chain

The date was 11th April 1644 when the town was the setting for a very much underplayed event that changed the whole course of the Civil War - the Battle of Selby.

The Governor of York, Colonel Bellasis had garrisoned what was then a little country town with a strong Royalist force of infantry and cavalry as well as six pieces of cannon but they were no match for a stronger Parliamentary army led by Lord Fairfax, his son Sir Thomas, and Sir John Meldrum.

On the previous day Lord Fairfax had issued a summons to the Royalists to yield the town as it was "a lost cause" but a defiant Bellasis angrily replied he would never deliver Selby to "a rebel".

Incensed by this response, at daybreak next morning Fairfax stormed the town which had been fortified by the Royalist soldiers with ditches, embankments, ramparts and barricades, supported by a bridge of boats across the River Ouse to maintain lines of communication with York and the East Riding.

The improvised fortifications proved no match for Sir Thomas Fairfax's cavalry who breached the barricades next to the River Ouse, thanks to a treacherous act. In charge of the defences was a certain Captain Wilson who deserted his post and, after the battle, was condemned to death for his cowardice by the council of war and duly shot.

Parliamentarian forces flooded into the town killing or wounding 1,000 of the defenders and capturing a further 1,800 including a large number of officers as well as a large amount of arms and some ships on the Ouse.

The remnants of Royalist cavalry counter charged the Parliamentarians and in the melée Bellasis suffered a sword and pistol shot wound before being captured.

He was described as a man "of great courage and valour who fought most gallantly for a town that was not really tenable", according to one contemporary observer.

Many of the Royalist foot soldiers who could, fled across the bridge of boats and ran as fast as their breastplates would allow, back towards the sanctuary of York. Not all of them made it. Some 500 of the fleeing fugitives were caught at Hemingbrough and in London it was reported that "divers slain, and lyes strewed in the Way to York for miles; others that fled to Pontefract we pursued to Ferry Bridge".

After the bloody conflict had raged through the streets for some nine hours all resistance had been crushed. The Royalists had been defeated and the morale of the officers and soldiers in their Yorkshire Army had been completely undermined by a plan which had backfired with disastrous consequences. By the time they came to do battle at Mars ton Moor they were already a spent force.

As one historian points out: "The Battle of Selby led directly to the siege of York and indirectly to the Battle of Mars ton Moor, so you could argue that Selby dealt THE fatal blow in the Civil War, certainly as far as Parliament was concerned".

and sea-coals for supplying the city of York and the adjacent counties by the river Ouse...'

By the eighteenth century the ferry here had gained considerably from this small port development and even earlier, in 1741, turnpiking of the road to Leeds had started. Indeed evidence collected by the promoters of a bridge suggests that the ferry was extremely busy with some 141,50 persons crossing annually of whom 36,614 were on horseback and about 29,000 beasts were also taken across the Ouse each year. These figures are based on a 1790 traffic census between 12 September and 12 October but are unlikely to be accurate as the bridge promoters simply multiplied the figures by 12! They also claimed that 'the Passage over the said Ferry, and every other Ferry upon the Ouse, *is at all Times, attended with Delay, in some Seasons dangerous, and at others impassable'.*

Ahead is the railway bridge originally built with twin cast iron bascules lifting at the centre of a 45 ft (14 metres) channel, by the Hull & Selby Railway between 1838 and 1840 in the face of opposition from river users who feared shoals and tidal problems. Opened for rail traffic on 1 July 1840 this continued to give service until 1 February 1891 when it was replaced by the present cast-iron structure. This bridge turns in a pivot-pier which is nearer the left bank and provides two opening of 60 feet (18 metres) and 54 feet (16 metres) though only the former is for navigation.

Once echoing to the clatter of East Coast main line trains between London and Edinburgh, traffic across the bridge was drastically reduced when

One of the bench ends in Hemingbrough Church

this line was diverted to enable the creation of the first new coal mine in the UK for decades which was seen as a response to widespread concern that the British mining industry was effectively shutting down, particularly following the defeat of the miners' strike (1984-85). Covering some 110 square miles (285km²), the Selby Complex featured some of the most advanced mining technology in Europe and in

Another bench end

1995 Wistow Colliery set the UK record for coal mined in one week – 200,743 tonnes. Over 3,000 miners plus contractors and ancillary staff were employed in the Selby Complex which closed on Friday 14 May 2004 due to rising costs caused by deteriorating geological conditions and the falling price of coal. In its final years the company listed a £30 million loss on the plant.

After about a quarter of a mile (0.3km) on the opposite side of the river is the entrance lock to the Selby Canal. Adjacent, facing both river and canal, is a not unattractive large modern fashionable flats development which has helped boost the town's population to around 13,000.

Misericord in Hemingborough Church

The Selby Canal was born out of competition between the Aire & Calder Navigation and the Leeds and Liverpool Canal who in 1771 prepared plans for continuation of their proposed cross-country canal from Leeds to Selby.

Originally the Aire and Calder Navigation came no nearer Selby than the course of the River Aire near West Haddlesey about five miles (8 km) away, but as trade increased, it was found expedient to avoid river impediments that occurred in several of the lower parts of the Aire, the most serious of which were between Knottingley and Haddlesey Lock. Immense profits were envisaged for anyone overcoming these problems, so it is not surprising that a scheme was advocated for making an extensive canal from Leeds to Selby. This was surveyed by a Mr Whitworth although the plan is believed to have originally been mooted in 1769 and a survey carried out by James Brindley. The route appears to have intended to adopt the course of the Selby Dam, starting a few miles above Selby. However, opposition from the powerful Aire and Calder Navigation Company squashed the proposal, and three years later – on 14th June 1774 – they obtained an Act 'for making a navigable canal from the River Aire at or near Haddlesey, to the River Ouse, at the old brick garth at Ousegate end within the township of Selby, and for other purposes'.

Costing £20,000, the 5½ mile (9km) canal built by the renowned engineer William Jessop, was opened on 24th April 1778 and brought considerable advantage to the town as an outlet for West Yorkshire manufacturers wanting to send goods by water to Hull, London and other parts, as well as shortening the distance between Leeds, York, Malton, Boroughbridge and other towns on the banks of the Ouse and its tributaries.

Initially cloth and agricultural produce was transported but with the booming West Yorkshire mining industry this soon gave way to 60 tonne coal barges. But the huge volume of traffic was its undoing since it also brought congestion and delays.

Having seen the benefits of expansionism, the Aire & Calder management in 1820 obtained an Act to build a new canal, which opened in 1826, from Knottingley to a junction with the River Ouse beyond Selby, at a little hamlet called Goole.

Two years later an Act of Parliament allowed Selby Canal to be widened and deepened with a new lock to the Ouse built at Selby. Despite this and further improvements in the 1830s, aided by the individual efforts of shippers like James Audus who operated nearly twenty schooners, the end result was inevitable. Usurped by the more direct route the keels heavily laden with woad, kelp, mustard seed, coal, and other material soon disappeared and served only to underline the local rhyme that:

> *'Selby was a seaport town when Goole was but a marsh,*
> *Now Goole it is a seaport and Selby fares the worse'.*

Continue along the metalled path, past some industrial works on your left and just after passing the derelict buildings which were once Cherry Orchard Farm, go through a way marked gate on your right on to the flood protection barrier and walk towards the swing bridge which carries the A63 Leeds to Hull road around the town and over the river as part of the £44 million Selby bypass. In July 2001 construction began on the Selby bypass having been authorised in 1993 for development. The bypass runs from the A19 at Barlby along the southern edge of Selby, connecting to the A63 at Thorpe Willoughby. The project was delayed due to technical difficulties with the bridge over the River Ouse but was eventually completed in July 2004.

At this stage it is possible to keep to the TransPennine Trail below the river all the way to Turnham Hall. If you want to keep a little closer to the river, then follow the adjacent way marked route on the flood protection barrier, leaving it before and rejoining it after the bridge; leaving it at Newlands farm buildings and rejoining after passing the final two houses past Newlands Farm; again leaving it at Turnham Hall to finally join the flood protection barrier at an intersection of ways in front of the hall and follow it for the rest of the walk to Hemingbrough. ➜ *page 90*

The winding river here with its soft banks is reminiscent of the River Severn and whilst everyone has heard of the Severn Bore, few if any seem to have heard of the Aegir. *Yet this tidal inrush of water which races up the Ouse when the strong flow of the river meets a high spring tide is markedly similar. In his famous book* Eboracum; or the History and Antiquities of the City of York, *published in 1736, the celebrated historian Francis Drake described it as 'a strange flow, or back current of water ... not ruled by the tides, called the Aegir. This makes a mighty noise as it approaches, insomuch as to be heard at some miles distance: and if it was not well known, would cause a great deal of terror to the country about it. The cause of this preternatural current I shall leave to the naturalists to determine. On the stretch of river hereabouts the whole moving wall of water travelling at around six miles an hour might reach a height of three feet and may well be followed by a succession of smaller waves'.*

For the uninitiated the occasional appearance of this phenomenon is just as awesome now as it was to the minds of those grizzly invaders from Scandinavia who venerated it as their sea god or Aegir

As you continue forward the skyline is punctured in the East by the cooling towers of Ferrybridge Electricity Generating Station, its brother at Eggborough in the South – both astride the River Aire which will later join the Ouse – and ahead the grandfather of them all, Drax.

Turnham Hall marks the point where the river formerly ran directly eastwards towards the village of Cliffe. The river now performs almost a complete circle over some three miles (5km) before reaching Landing Lane at Hemingbrough, affording fine views along the river as well as the beckoning spire of Hemingbrough. On the way it passes Newhay

Grange, once belonging to Drax priory, which occupied ground sited south of the Ouse until the river changed its course in the early Middle Ages, but in 1883 was absorbed by Hemingbrough.The name probably signifies the birig or burg of Hemma or Hemming, some very ancient landowner or chieftain, for Hemming was a common Norse name, but in the domesday Survey it is recorded as Hamiburg which according to historians' thoughts was an ancient tower or fort possibly near or on the site of the present church. But whether a Roman fort stood here or not, it is evident from the terminal of the name, that there was a burg or fortification of some kind early in the Saxon period, and tradition runs that Romans had a series of forts on the banks of the river, two miles (3km) or so apart, to keep navigation open, and that there was one here.

Landing Lane is the furthest turn off for the village and leads to the junction of Mill Lane with Main Street which joins the A63 Leeds to Hull road. A quicker route to view the church is to take an earlier marked footpath across a field at the point very close to (and directly opposite) Hemingbrough, where the river starts to bend. Walk directly towards the church and the footpath will take you over a footbridge and on to a lane, which runs down the side of the church into Main Street.

See box on page 91

For many years Hemingbrough could be reached by ferry from Newhay and one of the most interesting of our early chroniclers, Walter of Hemingbrough is believed to originate from here. His history, beginning with the Norman Conquest, is a rare work treasured in the British Museum.

Divine Right

The present course of the river slices off a tremendous sweep of land – the old channel can still be identified near Cliffe village – leaving Hemingbrough in splendid isolation but the tall needle-sharp 191-foot-high spire of St Mary the Virgin church still dominates the landscape.

Experts say that few spires are more finely built, but it has not been without its problems. In 1762 on 18th August it was struck by lightning, and so it was encased in scaffolding to enable repairs to be carried out. Work began on 16th September and was completed on 7th October, which became a red-letter day for the parish. Almost everyone, both young and old, climbed to the top and set foot on the coping-stone. To celebrate the event a new weathercock was put up, music was played at the top, and buckets of ale given by the village public houses were drawn up by rope to be sunk by the exuberant villagers. Being a prudent lot, they also took the precaution of putting an iron bar through the spire near its apex, and two large rings were fixed with a pulley in case they needed to haul anything up in the future. This proved to be particularly fortunate because on 27th May 1856 the spire was struck once again, and a Sheffield firm of architects called in for advice said that in their opinion the spire had been prevented from falling by an 18-foot iron spindle which they had found inserted in the upper part. If tradition has it then that lightning never strikes twice in the same place, Hemingbrough spire is testimony to the fallacy of tradition.

The first church that occupied the site was built in Saxon times, and is mentioned in domesday Book. But every trace of that edifice has disappeared, and of the Norman church that succeeded it there now remain only the two eastern-most bays on each side of the nave. The church appears to have been remodelled and enlarged in the thirteenth century, and traces of the Transitional style, which then prevailed, are visible in almost every part of the edifice. The transepts, originally built when the remodelling took place, were very considerably altered in the Perpendicular period, a clerestory being added, and the large five-light windows inserted in the north and south gables. Further enlargements were made in the fifteenth and sixteenth centuries by the addition of aisles to the chancel, and the widening of the north aisle of the nave. The beautiful tapering spire, was added in the fifteenth century.

Inside there are many things in which the curious will revel, particularly the ancient bench-ends with quaint heads, among them a jester with cap and bells; in the grotesque carving on four old panels of four monsters; a winged dragon with two heads, and an animal on a demon's mouth; a monkey putting its paw in the animal's mouth. On the end of one pew is carved a message which might prompt the reader to think he was being introduced to a Pope. It reads:

Greg'ry the 10th.	*In ninety-six.*	*From Hemingburgh.*
Of the ancient Race.	*The fifth of May,*	*To his celestial.*
Of Robinson's.	*Ag'd twice 18.*	*Retreat: 1696.*
Lies near this Place,	*Was call'd away,*	

8

Marriage of Waters

Hemingbrough to Boothferry

> **Start:** River Path at Landing Lane, Hemingbrough (Grid Ref: 669298).
> **Distance:** Approx 6 Miles/ 9.7Kilometres.
> **Terrain:** River Embankment.
> **Maps:** Explorer 291; Landranger 105.
> **Car Parking:** Roadside in Hemingbrough.
> **Public Transport:** No 4 Arriva Service Selby to Goole via Hemingbrough (check return times as service does not always start at Goole).
> **Refreshments:** The Crown, Fox & Pheasant in Hemingbrough; and bakery and village store; The Ferry Boat Inn, at Boothferry Bridge.

Hemingbrough once supported a variety of trades including farming, blacksmiths, brickworks, carriers, websters (weavers), maltsters, farriers, cattle dealers, and millers as can be seen in Bulmer's Directory of 1892. Now people commute not only to Selby and York but also to the larger cities of Leeds and Hull and even further afield for employment. In 2000 the last of fifteen working farms where wheat, oats, barley, turnips, and potatoes were chiefly grown moved outside the village. Most of these farms have been turned into building plots to cater for the greater number of new residents. In 1801 the population return Hemingbrough was home to 387 persons and in the census of 1991 the population had soared to 1,675.

Join the River Ouse from Landing Lane. If coming from Hemingbrough village, Landing Lane is the first turning right after the church walking along Main Street to the junction with Mill Lane which bears left. Walk along the river embankment as it swings south for a little over a mile (1¾ km) to reach the confluence with the River Derwent at Barmby-on-the-Marsh. Here there is a tidal barrage. Just before the barrage come off the embankment and go to the left of marshy ground, which is fenced off. At the end of this section turn right and follow the path around to cross the barrage and the Derwent. ➔ *page 96*

Formerly a river port with a sail-cloth and rope-making industry using locally grown flax, Barmby-on-the Marsh now survives as a collection of picturesque cottages and imposing houses, although the population has declined from around 500 in the eighteenth century to about 300 nowadays. The river used to be busy too with grain and other crops taken to market and mills, with coal coming on the return journey. It even had salmon fishing and was served by two ferries – one across the River Derwent and another over the Ouse to Long Drax. – which in the 1790`s were in the hands of the Earl of Beverley, lord of the manor of Airmyn and lessee of the Bishop of Durham.

Opinions differ about the origin of its name. Some authorities claim it was probably the 'farmstead of the children', that is one held jointly by a number of heirs, derived from the Old Scandinavian barn *and* by*, alternatively a farmstead owned by a Scandinavian called* Barni *or* Bjarni. *The Old English* mersc – marsh – *appears to have been added later as the name progressed through* Barnebic *and* Barmby-on-Derwent *to its present form.*

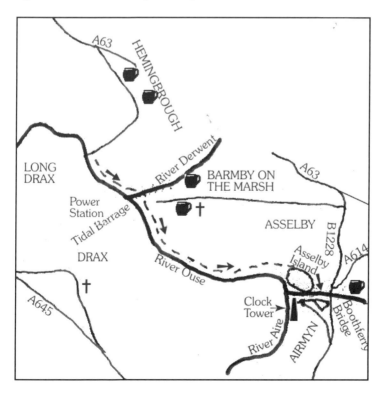

The village once had a three day horse racing festival and Barmby Feast was held annually. In winter the surrounding marshland often flooded and provided lots of opportunities for ice skating!

Originally a barn with a brick eastern tower added later, the ancient church of St Helen's has in its churchyard St Helen's Well, a spring rich in iron. Nearby is St Peter's well, rich in sulphur. Both were a boon to the villagers in 1854 when they helped to protect the population from a cholera outbreak.

Here at Barmby the Ouse now consumes the River Derwent, whose waters started their peculiar and erratic 75-mile journey from its source where it gurgles out of a bog some 850 feet above sea level on Allerston High Moor. Geologists tell us that the Derwent originally flowed direct to the North Sea in the vicinity of Scarborough, which would have made it a very short river of about seven miles. To this day there is a flood-relief channel known as 'the Sea Cut' which carries excess flood waters from the river direct to the sea. The Derwent assumed its present southward peregrination at the end of the Ice Age and remained a 'natural river' until the early-eighteenth century, when a series of locks and weirs were constructed to make the river navigable from its mouth for 38 miles to Malton.

Yorkshire Water Authority classes the Derwent as a 'drinking river' since it supplies water to one-seventh of the population of the county and drains a tenth of its area.

In an endeavour to provide for future increases in water consumption, a £1m tidal barrage was built across the mouth of the river to exclude the twice-daily salty intrusions of the Ouse from a previously tidal stretch.

Completed and commissioned in May 1975, the great 14-ton concrete sluice gates and piled approaches topped by coloured navigation lights sit uneasily in the verdant banks of the Ouse, for it has been the subject of considerable controversy. Farmers along the Derwent contend that higher river levels lead to water-logging, flooding and sometimes destruction of hay crops. On the other hand, anglers now get good catches of roach and dace and even the occasional trout in former barren waters whilst salmon have been sighted. Mayflies, snails and caddis flies – indicative of good, clean water – have moved in, as well as colonies of swallows, stock doves and pied wagtails. Herbs, grass and shrubs are also thriving on its banks.

Without doubt the tidal barrage is a great civil engineering feat in the creation of a new channel, installation of complex electronics for automatic operation and remote sensors.

Also provided are a car park, picnic site and toilets.

Looming over everything like a giant industrial cathedral on the western bank is Drax Power Station with the tallest chimney in the country – 44,000 tonnes of reinforced concrete some 850 feet (259 metres) high. Constructed in August 1968, it casts its long shadow over the twelve cooling towers each 375 feet high(114 metres) and 312 feet (95 metres) wide at the base- big enough to hold the dome of St Paul's Cathedral- in which 160 million litres of water drawn from the River Ouse are cooled. The water has to be very pure, otherwise during the continuous boiling and condensing process the boiler tubes- enough to stretch the 300 miles (483 km) from London to Newcastle -would rapidly 'fur up'. Water from the Ouse is made a thousand times more pure for this purpose in a water-treatment plant before it is used to make up losses in the main boilers and one circulating pump can move 880 tonnes of water in one minute – enough to fill 2,700 baths! This great behemoth supplies seven percent of the nation's power from its six generators each of which has an output of 660 MW. Every unit has ten pulverising mills each capable of crushing 36 tonnes of coal an hour and around 3,800 tones of coal an hour are move around by conveyors.

Across the river are the villages of Drax, and Long Drax, in bygone days a regular

The Airmyn clock tower

calling point for passenger steam packets serving Goole, Hull, Selby and York.

According to the Dictionary of English Place-Names *in* Domesday Book (1086) *it was recorded as* Drac *but by the eleventh century it was* Drachs *meaning `The portages or places where boats are dragged overland or pulled up from the water' derived from the Old Scandinavian* drag.

Characterised now by rustic quiet it was once a centre of ecclesiastical life of considerable importance which is reflected in the Norman church of St Peter and St Paul.

A striking feature of the church is the fifteenth century clerestory of the nave, like a continuous arcade with eight three-light windows each side, adorned outside with a great show of gargoyles and fine battlements. Under the windows inside is a fine sculpture gallery of saints and apostles, abbots, bishops and kings – relics of the priory which once stood nearby.

Bench-ends are valuable specimens of late-medieval carving, bringing a quaintness and originality to rival the grotesqueness of gargoyles on the clerestory. One, a passable carving of a large drake, is claimed by antiquaries to be a pun on the name of the place – Drax or Drakes. On other bench ends are conventional designs with such oddities as a pig playing bagpipes to a dancer, and a kneeling figure upside down with a sheep's head above it. Another, depicting a giant in a crown with three feathers leading a boy by a chain, is less likely to be considered idiosyncratic by boys attending a big school which has grown out of one founded here in 1667 by Charles Reed – a benefactor whose story is not unlike that of Moses. He it was who provided the funds for the establishment of 'The school and master's house, with the alms houses adjacent....in the reign of Charles the Second'.

| See box on page 98 |

Having crossed the barrage, over to the right is a gate. Go through this and continue on along the embankment, passing two houses on your left. For the next three miles the Ouse, swollen and widened by Derwent's waters, surges eastwards as it prepares for yet another merger of waters in the secrecy of a hinterland untrammelled by roads, hamlets or even farmsteads.

Continue forward. Bridge supports on both banks and the brick house- recently modernised to look less Victorian – formerly occupied by the controller, are all that remain to remind you that the old Hull & Barnsley Railway bridged the Ouse here with a 360 foot lattice-girder structure in 1885 to carry across trains laden with coal before both became uneconomical. ➜ *page 101*

Asselby, or Aschhilebi as it was in Domesday Book (1086) was the 'farmstead of a man called Askell' and is the little village about a mile distant on your left, which has given its name to a wooded island around which the swirling waters of Rivers Ouse and Aire engage in an intimate marital ritual from which the Ouse emerges as master.

`Aire' or 'Air' is the ancient British word for 'bright', but the inky cesspool that drags its highly flavoured waters into the Ouse should blush with shame on hearing its name. The crystal waters that gush from the foot of Malham Cove in the heart of the Pennine dales may be

Carved bench ends in Drax church

worthy of such a tribute, but then they have not yet suffered the indignities of industrialization which the river receives on its 70-mile journey to the confluence.

Looking down the throat of the River Aire is the village of Airmyn, a name said to be a corruption of Aire Mouth, recorded as Ermenie in Domesday Book (1086). Here is the home of one of Yorkshire's most unusual monuments, now nearly a century and a half old. It is an

Studies in Success

Working in the riverside fields early in the seventeenth century, some Drax labourers were distracted by a faint, feeble, tremulous wail. Astonished by so strange a sound in so sequestered a spot, they investigated and found

among some reeds a fine, healthy infant abandoned to his fate. The little lad, for it proved to be a boy, was taken to the workhouse and cared for there, eventually being baptized by the name of Charles Reed in allusion to the reeds amongst which he was found. Every effort to trace his parents failed, and so the boy was reared on charity. He soon began to show such an acute intelligence and talent that he was sent to the village school, where he quickly outstripped his teachers in both grammatical and arithmetical prowess. His spirit, prudence, perseverance and enterprise provided abundant proof that he was destined to be no ordinary character. When he grew up and learned of his back-

Bell and clock on Drax school

ground, he resolved to leave Drax, where he was forever liable to taunts and the finger of ungenerous scorn. He asked the parochial protectors to get him a job on a merchant ship, and he left for the East Indies full of undying gratitude for their past kindness and a resolve to repay his debt if opportunity ever presented itself. Arriving in Madras, he was lucky enough to find a job with British traders and a chance to demonstrate his diligence and integrity. Through successive promotions he amassed both power and wealth, but he never forgot his humble start in life. He used some of his fortune in 1667 to endow a school at Drax, with an injunction that the boys who attended should take turns at sweeping out the schoolhouse every Saturday afternoon, with a sixpenny fine being the penalty for failure to comply.

elegant clock-tower, which has strangers guessing when they first see it on a bend in the village street.

'Where is the church?' they invariably enquire when they see the steeple-like structure with its spiky pyramid roof on four steep gables topping the nearby trees and cottages. To add to their consternation, the timepiece has only three faces on the four sides.

A Bradford architect, W. J. Lockwood, built the clock in 1865 with voluntary subscriptions totalling almost £700, as a testimonial to George Percy, Earl of Beverley and Lord of the Manor, for his many acts of kindness and consideration towards the tenants of his estates. Although the cost of the tower was covered by public donations, there is a popular belief in the village that the methods used to raise the cash came pretty near to compulsion. One farmer, however, at Little Airmyn across the river, with typical Yorkshire stubbornness refused to

More carved bench ends

contribute, which is why there is no clock face on the side seen from that direction. For everyone it provides a useful landmark and for those fortunate enough to see the faces a reliable record of the time, since the only occasion the clock has stopped was when the hands were frozen in one particularly severe winter.

St James Chronicle or the British Evening Post of 19th March 1765 carried an advertisement announcing the sailing of vessels from Stanton's Wharf, London to 'Armine'. Prior to the opening of Goole by the Aire and Calder Navigation Company, vessels traded regularly from London up the Aire to Leeds, but from the advertisements it would appear that Airmyn was a port of discharge and loading for vessels sailing at least every eight days.

Apart from a dominating position at the confluence of two major rivers, Airmyn was also on the threshold of Boothferry; this, the longest survivor of all the major Ouse ferries, ceased operating only in 1929 on completion of the steel-girder swing bridge which still spans the Ouse here.

Schemes to replace the ferry at Booth were proposed as early as 1907 when the Aire & Calder Navigation favoured a transporter bridge. Naturally suspicious of the whole idea the Ouse Navigation Trustees opposed it on the grounds that it would be 'dangerous and inconvenient to Navigation.' After many delays the West Riding County Council agreed to build the bridge about 350 yards (320 metres) below the old ferry and proposed a rolling bascule type which was then enjoying popularity with civil engineers. In 1925 the necessary Act of Parliament was obtained but a more orthodox swinging span design was chosen.

The Cleveland Bridge and Engineering Company started work building the 698-foot (213 metre)-long bridge in January 1926. Completed at a cost of £105,235 three years later it was officially opened on Thursday 18th July. Power to operate the bridge crossed the river on tall masts from Goole to a sub-station on the north side of the river because Howden was not yet electrified. When opened the bridge releases a navigation channel of 125 feet (38 metres) for ships.

The river at this point runs very rapidly with the ebb tide, and the huge flat-bottomed ferry used for carrying horses, vehicles and cattle across the swollen stream must have been a perpetual source of jeopardy both for users and for other river traffic. Legend has it that *somewhere here stood the cottage of Booth, the ferryman who bequeathed us his name – prior to being called Booth's Ferry in 1651 it appears to have been known in 1550 as Botheby after a family who originated from somewhere called Boothby. However ownership of the ferry was in the hands of the powerful prince-bishops of Durham, who leased it out. Best-known lessees and operators were the Wells family who prospered through the large coaching-establishment and inn which they maintained here. Ever-mindful of opportunities for expansion, John Wells bought shares in several Goole ships and was an early director of Goole Steam Shipping Company.*

Originally Booth Ferry House had stood on the northern bank of the Ouse, but the nineteenth-century house – where the Aire and Calder contract for the first Goole docks was signed – was on the opposite side. The ferry in those days was the key to the district. Consequently, until the 1870s the Ferry Boat inn on the northern bank was the departure-point for a horse-omnibus which connected the Ouse steam-packet with the town of Howden, a couple of miles away, where travellers could give thanks for a safe journey. Here for two nights in May 1699 stayed the enigmatic Thomas Surbey who had been engaged by York Corporation to survey the river. He discovered the hazardous shoals near Asselby and at Boothferry which he resolved to eliminate by cutting a new channel around them, a project which never came to fruition.

With the two bridges in sight – Boothferry carrying A614 and Ouse Bridge the M62, over the river – almost as if they are one on top of the other, the embankment meets a lane. Come off the embankment and walk along the lane to join the A614 where you turn right to cross the bridge and enjoy dramatic views of road traffic apparently in the sky as it traverses the river on the elongated arch of the M62 Ouse Bridge.

9

Bartholomew's Vineyard

Boothferry to Swinefleet

Start: Boothferry Bridge A614 (Grid Ref (734263).
Distance: Approx 8 Miles/12 Kilometres.
Terrain: Level towpath and roads.
Maps: Explorer 291; Landranger 106.
Car Parking: Lane leading to Booth on north side of bridge.
Public Transport: No 8 Selby to Drax via Airmyn (Arriva), 156 Goole to North Ferriby via Ferry Boat Inn (East Yorkshire) and 357 Goole to Scunthorpe (Sweyne Coaches); all may be of help in planning this journey.
Refreshments: Several in Goole; Blacksmiths Arms, and Sotherton Arms, Hook, Kings Head, Swinefleet.

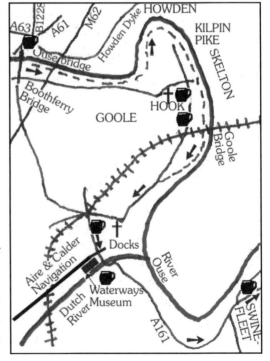

Having crossed the bridge, turn immediately left down the embankment through a break in the fence, to join the riverside path as it makes a curve of about 3½ miles (5½ km) to the built up area on the riverside at Goole. ➜ *page 105*

The route takes you under the M62 trans-Pennine motorway which links the two ports of Liverpool and Hull. A graceful, stilted arch rises between Airmyn and Hook to lift the six-lane highway a hundred feet above the river before de-

scending with equal elegance near Howden Dyke. The £10-million bridge took more than three years to complete because of complex subsoil problems which had to be overcome before a firm foundation could be reached. With a gentle gradient of about 3%, the bridge is 4,396 feet (1,340 metres) long, although this extends to 7,087 feet (2,160 metres) when the approach spans, which include crossing the A614, are taken into consideration. This marvel of concrete and steel technology swallowed 14,400 cubic yards of concrete in the deck slabbing and another 22,200 cubic yards in the supporting piers.

Despite the unrelenting hubbub of traffic high above, this stretch of river is a rambler's paradise with grassy embankments bordered by whispering reeds lapped by gentle waters providing a habitat in which numerous water-loving birds flourish.

As you reach the top of the finger of the first bend before turning south towards Hook, you can see Howden Dyke on the northern bank. Once a hamlet of farmhands and labourers at the riverside fertilizer factory, it has become a mini-port extending along the riverside towards

Aerial view of Howden Dyke

the hamlets of Kilpin Pike and Skelton, with concrete jetties, ware-houses, chemical works, cranes, fork-lift trucks, lorries, conveyors, pal-lets and all the other industrial impedimenta which the arriving and departing coasters demand. As early as 1853 a Mr Anderton dissolved bones and made super phosphate and other fertilizers at Howden Dyke on the site of a disused tannery. And on one occasion at least a shipload of mummified cats was imported into Hull from Egypt to be sold as or-ganic fertilizer, along with the regular supplies of guano and bone-meal both home-produced and imported. In 1910 five sloops – the Cupro, Hydro, Sulpho, Phospho *and* Nitro, *with carrying-capacities from 90 to 150 tons, were regular visitors to the wharf. These wooden craft carried a foresail and mainsail, the pride of the little fleet being the* Hydro *which boasted an additional topsail and a very canny skipper who, although unable to read and write, knew every yard of the Humber and Ouse from Hull to York like the back of his hand. They took out fertilizer to landings on the Ouse and Trent until 1935 when they were sold.*

Puncturing the horizon beyond is the Minster tower of St Peter & St Paul at Howden. Before it achieved ecclesiastical prominence Howden

Howden Market Square

attracted merchants from as far away as London to its fair which had been granted by King John in 1200. By the end of the fourteenth century Howden, with just four hundred taxpayers, was the fifth largest settlement in the East Riding of Yorkshire

Two centuries later the situation had changed dramatically, with the neglect and deterioration of land-drainage leading to the abandonment of many small settlements in the locality as well as closures of a sacking-factory in the 1830s, tanneries in the 1850s and a short-lived flax-factory in the late 1860s.

The only commercial event to prosper was the traditional horse-fair. In May 1856, according to the Howdenshire Gazette 'not less than 10,000 attended ... the town literally swarmed with thieves, among whom the Manchester Swell Mob was in great force'. In August 1864 the Great Yorkshire Show was held here, which resulted in 'iron bedsteads being imported in large numbers, so that the usual amount of room occupied by the old four-posters may be made available' for the influx of visitors. But it was the horse-fair that was the chief attraction and it soon became the town's most important event. In 1807 it was described as 'indisputably the largest fair for horses in the kingdom ... being attended by all the principal dealers from London, Edinburgh, and from several of the great towns in England. It may be estimated that 4,000 horses are every day exposed for sale, 16,000 being disposed of at the last fair, altogether worth not less than £200,000.' So great was the horde of visitors that the inns were full to capacity, and in some the customers 'were obliged to sleep three in a bed and in others the lodgers absolutely covered the floor'.

See box on page 106

As you approach Hook, which is almost encircled by the river, you pass Hook Hall, built in 1743 by Admiral Frank Sotheron who was said to have sailed with Nelson, and then new housing. Still following the embankment, you come to an open grassed area, planted with trees: ahead the land is overgrown. Walk diagonally across this area to a gate, which will take you to a fenced path behind more houses. Continue along this path, behind the back gardens of the riverside houses in Hook. ➔ *page 107*

The burgeoning village of Hook no longer owes its importance to the river ferry from Howden Dyke, which began to be a regular crossing-place in 1214. But it does have a claim to fame in the lowly

Rags to Riches

From this former hub of horse-trading emerged a stable-lad who became Prime Minister of Lucca and Parma, was covered with decorations and created Baron Ward. Born in 1810 the son of a poor stable-helper, Tom Ward received only a little education before starting life in the training-stables of a former stable-lad, then at the zenith of fame and fortune – Bob Ridsdale of Merton. Ward was sent to Vienna in charge of some thoroughbreds and from under-groom advanced to become confidential and chief adviser to the Duke of Lucca. By a diplomatic move he restored the flagging fortunes of the Duchy of Lucca, for which he was rewarded by being made minister of finance, created baron and decorated with the Order of St Louis and also the Order of St Joseph. Through Ward's machinations the Grand Duke of Tuscany's son, Charles Albert, was placed on the throne of Parma as Charles II.

Yorkshire shrewdness, sharp intelligence, bold character, a sense of honour, frankness and native wit combined in Ward to create what Metternich described as a 'heaven-born minister', whilst Lord Palmerston pronounced Ward to be 'one of the most remarkable men he ever met'. In his high station and prosperity Ward never forgot his family or his native home, and he paid annual visits to Howden, bringing gifts and taking York hams back as presents for Court nobles. He retired eventually to a farm outside Vienna, in marked contrast to his old master, who, after earning thousands of pounds through ownership of both Derby and St Leger winners, was found dead in a hay-loft with just three halfpence in his pocket.

bellcote church of St Mary's with a stained-glass window said to be unique.

Resembling a vivid page from a picture book, it depicts Queen Victoria near the close of her long life, visiting the wounded of the South African War. Watched by a nurse and sundry ladies, the Queen sits in her wheel-chair proffering to a bed-ridden soldier a bunch of golden daffodils held by one other lady clad in a fur-collared mantle. In charge of the royal party is an officer in the brilliant blue uniform of the Guards.

As if reflecting this royal reverence a notice in the entrance porch warns visitors:

'Enter this door.   As if the choir.
As if the floor.   In robes of fire.
Within were gold,   Were singing here.
And every wall.   Nor shout nor rush.
Of jewels all.   But hush.
Of worth untold;   For GOD is near'.

Some authorities claim that Hook takes its name from the bend in the river but others claim it is derived from a certain John de Huck who was granted a chantry chapel by the Abbot of Selby in 1214. A Poll Tax account of the district in 1317 shows that of 1500 men, over 1200 were accounted for by just four names – 554 were called John, 421 William (tribute perhaps to a successful plunderer), 156 Robert and 155 Thomas. The next two most common were Richard and Adam but there was no woman called Eve.

As you leave the last houses of Hook and approach the railway bridge across the Ouse, depending upon the time of year it may be preferable to walk on the left hand side of the flood wall on the riverbank; the path may be very overgrown on the right hand side. ✛

Between Hook and Goole the Barnsley branch of the former North Eastern Railway finds its way impeded by the river which is about 750 feet (228 metres) wide now. This problem was overcome in 1869 with a massive cast-iron double-line bridge, – one of the finest examples of its kind in the world.- built by John Butler & Co of Stanningley Ironworks, Leeds. The 830-foot-long (253 metres) structure, some 60 feet(18 metres) high, has a giant swinging span of 250 feet, (76 metres) weighing 670 tons. This ponderous link can be swung open or closed by its hydraulic mechanism in the short space of fifty second. Depending on who you talk to it is known either as 'Goole', 'Hook' or 'Skelton Bridge'.

Walk underneath and a hundred yards further downstream where the navigational jurisdiction of British Waterways over the River Ouse ends and the mantle passes to Associated British Ports, an inscribed iron post commemorates the upper limits of an improvements scheme carried out in 1886 by the Aire & Calder Navigation Company. Continue forward on the embankment to pass the peaceful landscaped gardens of Goole Cemetery which back on to the river. Further along as you walk parallel to the Hook Road, the embankment becomes more of a promenade as you join the manicured Hook Road Riverside Garden with footpaths designed to encourage leisurely strolls to view the scenic qualities of the river.

At the end of the Riverside gardens you pass the memorial garden to seamen: here you leave the river to turn right along North Street. Go up to the roundabout where you take the second exit, Stanhope Street, leading to the docks and the heart of Goole. At the T-junction turn left down Lower Bridge Street. Walk straight ahead, crossing two bridges. At

Memorial to Sailors on the river bank at Goole

the far end of Bridge Street you will cross the Aire and Calder Navigation and the Dutch River between which is sandwiched Vermuyden Terrace, home of the Yorkshire Waterways Museum established in 1995 and extended in 2001. More than 7000 documents, photographs and artifacts comprise an extensive collection whose largest object is the working Tom Pudding tug *Wheldale*. → *page 112*

'It is singular that in most modern maps the town of Goole is not laid down. Yet it stands on the banks of the Ouse, two-hundred yards from the point where the Dutch River empties itself therein – a striking instance of the rapid advance of British commerce – a small village risen to the dignity and importance of a considerable shipping port; and at the same time the very boys that play at marbles in the streets call to mind the digging of the foundations'. Thus wrote Sir George Head in A Home Tour through the Manufacturing Districts of England *in 1836. His surprise was not unreasonable, because until the 1820s Goole was no more than a hamlet beside the Ouse, with a population of 450 surviving by digging peat besides growing flax and potatoes. True there was a staith on the river bank – Murham Staith, and ships averaged about five calls a year to load potatoes. Opinions as to the origin of the name vary, but the word 'goul' meant 'drain' when the Dutch engineer Cornelius Vermuyden was called in by Charles I to drain 24,000 acres of Hatfield Chase bog land in 1620. Vermuyden's original plan resulted in flooding at Fishlake, Sykehouse and Snaith to the anger and anguish*

Commemorative plate showing
the Goole Coat of Arms

of the farming communities. Sporadic local rioting resulted in a judgement in 1633 compelling the creation of a new channel from the River Don at Newbridge to an outfall in the Ouse rather than the Aire. The Dutch River, as it was aptly named, was built at a cost of £30,000, but by 1639 Vermuyden was in gaol for debt.

In the West Yorkshire hinterland, as the manufacturing towns experienced the birth-pangs of industrialization, the enterprising directors of the Aire and Calder Navigation Company, established by Act of Parliament in 1699, pressed forward with attempts to improve the network of waterways which served the region. Dubbed by one cynical observer 'The fourth estate of the realm', the formidable company decided to make Goole the outlet to the Ouse tideway of a new canal. The navvies descended on the little hamlet and the canal from Knottingley was officially and ceremoniously opened in July 1826.

'... an immense number of spectators assembled at Ferrybridge to witness the departure of the opening procession ... decorated with national flags...banners, attended by several bands of music, and followed by a train of between forty and fifty sail vessels...the procession entered the Barge Dock at Goole under a royal salute of twenty-one guns fired from twelve pounders stationed on the pier for the occasion and amidst the huzzas of thousands of spectators...'

Almost immediately the population of Goole shot up from 450 to 1,671; it had multiplied a further seven times by 1851.

The Undertakers of the Aire and Calder Navigation, as they morbidly styled themselves, were benevolent dictators of the port they owned. Amongst the many structures which they built of red bricks yielded by the clay lands of the vicinity was Banks Hotel, later renamed Lowther Hotel (now seriously dilapidated) in honour of Sir John Lowther who served for several years as the company chairman. In an upstairs banqueting room that once served as the boardroom of the company is a superb mural from about 1830 showing sailing ships and warehouses bearing testimony to former greatness.

In 1828 they built a Custom House and 'a number of handsome houses for the agents and officers of the establishment flanked by the river locks'. A total of 178 dwellings had been constricted by 1829 as the proprietors pursued a policy 'according to which all the buildings are to be erected of fine brick or stone, and covered with blue slate; and if this be carried into effect, the town...will, in point of elegance and uniformity, be the handsomest in the North of England'.

A Hull customs official was so moved by the transformation that he wrote:

> *'The machinery and docks are extremely complete,*
> *And the offices remarkable neat;*
> *With the elegant stores of that size.*
> *That the craft of the river may unload or discharge.*
> *In the dock of the warehouse, unusually large:*
> *Which excites a degree of surprise.*
> *No little huts just raised from the ground.*
> *Nor vulgar red tiles on the roofings are found;*
> *But elegance decks each design.*
> *The streets are well formed for prospect or health;*
> *And the whole proves the builders are rolling in wealth,*
> *From the fairest indelible sign.*
> *The gardens are stored with abundance of good,*
> *From honest industry, for pleasure or food,*
> *And the sight is a feast to behold...'*

Between 1843 and 1848 the stately and well-proportioned church of St John was erected by the canal authorities, and fifty-two guineas were donated annually 'so that the performance of Divine worship according to the Rites of the Church of England [might] thereby be provided in perpetuity. A grant of a weekly market was obtained and considerable help given in the foundation of a school, soup-kitchen for the poor, literary and scientific institute and even ... a regatta'.

Taking advantage of the vending facilities in 1849 a Goole man on discovering that his wife was unfaithful put a halter around her waist and led her into the market where she was sold by public auction. Bidding started at three pence and reached five shillings and nine pence at which price she was sold to her lover.

To protect navigation property a fire-engine was maintained, and until the 1870s the Aire and Calder Undertakers ministered to the needs of Goole citizens from the cradle to the grave. But the Public

Health Act of 1872 which proposed the setting up of a sanitary authority pricked the bubble of fatherly overseer. The Undertakers petitioned that they might assume this responsibility, claiming that they had expended more than £1,250,000 on the creation of Goole, which they had served well. They omitted to say that it had served them well too. The petition failed, and the 7,792 citizens found they had taken the first faltering step towards a new independent existence of fending for themselves on the way to becoming the tenth port in England with a population now around eighteen thousand. And looking down on it all like a benign godfather is Goole's giant water-tower – allegedly the biggest in England – some 145 feet (44 metres) high and with a capacity of 750,000 gallons.

A visit to the town museum reveals that despite the best efforts of the proprietors the Aire & Calder Navigation the port attributes its foundation to a whale, whose jaw bones are preserved there. Apparently a young bottle-nosed whale, blinded by river silt, presumably in the wake of shoals of salmon that migrated from the coast in vast numbers during the early nineteenth century, strayed up the Ouse. Whether by

The 'Tom Pudding' barge system invented by William Bartholemew for coal transport

accident or design, the unfortunate creature was killed and ancient Anglo-Saxon law was invoked. This stated that 'Where a bishop has his seat, that place is a city, and where a whale is killed, there is a port'. Everyone was in accord and Goole was allowed to develop thanks to this providential act of God. Thus it was divine intervention rather than

*digging a ditch that kick-started the creation of the port – although other
views tend to prevail!*

See box on page 113

Having passed the Dutch river, turn left into Old Goole following the
A161 until you come to Humber Street with St Mary's Church on its
corner. Turn left down this street and walk to the end to rejoin the
river embankment to the right. Now continue along the
embankment past vast stretches of reeds separating you from the
river to Swinefleet with its pantiled rooftops standing out against
high-banked dykes. → *page 114*

About 1195 the village was called Swyneflet *derived from the Old
English* swin *and* fleot – *the stretch of river where pigs are kept – which
suggests that it may owe its name to pig farming. Local theorists however ascribe the name* Swinefleet *to the visit of an invading Danish
chieftain called* Sweyne *who anchored his fleet in the river at this point.
The personal name* Sweyne *might be acceptable, but `fleot` was generally a stream.*

*One distinction Swinefleet can claim without fear of contradiction is
its title as the 'Metropolis of Marshland`. Early in the nineteenth cen-
tury it was roamed by so many thieves, burglars and robbers that in
1812 the residents banded together to form the Marshland Association
for Prosecution of Felons. Individuals unable to afford the prosecution
of the increasing number of criminals joined this vigilante group which
used to meet at the* Ship Inn *in Swinefleet. Their existence seems to re-
flect the sledgehammer cracking a nut syndrome if a handbill they
issued in 1844 is any guide:*

*'Four Pounds Reward. In consequence of the numerous petty thefts
and depredations committed upon property left in the closes the
members of this association have resolved to prosecute all persons who
can be found guilty of such offences. Notice is hereby given that
whoever will give information so as to lead to the apprehension of the
person or persons who a short time ago cut from a sheep net in the
pastures at Armin the property of Mr Gallon, a member of this
association, several yards of the bottom line, supposed to be taken for
ass tether, on conviction, receive £2 from Mr Gallon and £2 from Mr
William Smith, the association treasurer'.*

*The rich flat alluvial land across the river once formed part of the
Manor of Howden, owned by King Edward the Confessor following the*

Tale of Tom Puddings

The port of Goole – founded on coal, created as a coal terminal, flourished because of coal and almost died because of coal, for until the First World War coal was by far the biggest egg in Goole's basket.

The emergent railway companies coveted the coal-trade and were greedily grabbing bigger and bigger chunks of it. Without some radical innovation in water transport, the railways were all set to monopolize the business.

But they had not reckoned with the inventive genius of William H. Bartholomew, who at twenty-two years of age had been appointed resident engineer of the Aire and Calder. He modestly described his breakthrough in a paper presented to the Fourth International Congress on Inland Navigation held in Manchester in 1890.

'One special feature in the traffic on the Aire & Calder Navigation is that of the conveyance by what are termed 'compartments' of minerals, mainly coal. The 'compartment' boats are constructed of steel and are 16 ft by 20 ft by 8 ft deep, and carry 35 tons each. Each of these barges is provided with buffers, and the whole are attached together like railway waggons, a wire rope on each side connects with the tug, and enables the crew of the latter to steer them. Thus no crews are required on the 'compartments', and a great saving in transit time is thereby effected. At Goole are two hydraulic hoists and here the train is broken up, and the 'compartment' boats lifted singly out of the water in a 'cage' provided for the purpose, and the contents tipped into the sea-going vessel. The 'compartments' can be covered over and used for the conveyance of damageable traffic when required. They travel in trains varying from 10 to 30 at a time, but 700 tons is regarded as a very convenient train'.

In its heyday, Goole was receiving what appeared to be an unending stream of these craft loaded to the brim with black nuggets; over 1½ million tons passed through the port in the best year. It was this that elevated Goole to the pinnacle of success. Elevation was indeed the keynote, for the barge hoists, or tipplers as they are sometimes called, which ensured a speedy turn-round for barges and coasters alike, were undoubtedly the forerunners of modern mechanical-handling techniques. They also provided the inspiration for the wag who not inaptly nicknamed the port 'Bartholomew's Vineyard'.

Soon after the strange new craft were introduced, they became known colloquially as 'Tom Puddings'. Several theories exist to account for the novel name, but the most popular explanation suggests they are so called because, when they are unladen and stand high above the water line, they resemble old-fashioned Yorkshire pudding tins. 'Tin' was simply corrupted to 'Tom', and the two words were reversed.

Norman Conquest and was in the hands of the Saltmarshe family for over 700 years. Phillip Saltmarshe, when Bishop of Ripon built the hall here and Reverend John Saltmarshe, one of Cromwell's chaplains was of this family. He was a religious fanatic and a prolific author who predicted the day and hour of his death to his wife and other people. True to his word – unlike Hannah Beedham at Kelfield – he died on the day fixed upon and an account of his life and last moments are quaintly described as ' in the presence of many godly people of Quality'.

Unloading cargo vessels in Goole docks

The 3,268-acre estate of some 15 farms, woodlands and sporting rights was acquired for over £2.5 million in 1993 by a trust formed by the tenant farmers.

The river below Goole increasingly savours more of the sea than an inland waterway. When the tide is at flood there is a great stretch of water flush with the flood banks, spreading without break from shore to shore in some places a half a mile or more wide. As you approach Swinefleet, you have to leave the embankment on to a roadside path to cross a dyke. As it reaches Swinefleet, you can see High Street to your left. It has been blocked off from the A161. Turn down here if you want to visit the *Kings Head* for some refreshment. (The bus stop is at the junction of High Street and Church Lane).

10

Time and Tide

Swinefleet to Adlingfleet Ings

Start: Top of High Street, Swinefleet (Grid Ref 767222).
Distance: Approx 7 miles/11km kilometres.
Terrain: River embankment and roads. After Ousefleet the path
can be very overgrown and muddy especially where it passes
through a Conservation area for birds and grazing marsh.
Maps: Explorer 291; Landranger 106.
Car Parking: Roadside at the top of High Street, where it is
blocked off from the A161.
Public Transport: 357 Goole to Scunthorpe via Swinefleet and
Blacktoft Sands, Sweyne Coaches).
Refreshments: Kings Head, Swinefleet, Half Moon, Reedness,
Hope &Anchor Blacktoft.

*Sandwiched between Low Street which carries the A161 main road
from Goole and the now rapidly burgeoning river is High Street,
Swinefleet which was once an important ferry crossing. This was struck
by a great tragedy on 21st September, 1735 when, as Whitgift parish
register tells us 'The ferry boat at Swinefleet was overset with 15
persons on it, 14 of whom miserably perished in ye river'.*

*The river here was once notorious for the number of ships lost on
the curve of the river known as the 'Swinefleet Bend'. This was
eliminated in 1884 with the Ouse (Lower) Improvement Bill which
strengthened the banks and retaining walls.*

Whilst it is possible to walk on the river embankment from the
top of High Street near the Kings Head, the path behind the
housing is very overgrown with vegetation and walking can
be difficult and unpleasant. The easier (and preferred) alternative is
to walk down High Street, parallel to the river and on to the
Reedness road.

Just past Sweyne Garth, which is a cul-de-sac, there is an entrance
to a field with a bungalow on its right hand corner near the road.
Diagonally cross this field to the river embankment and from here
continue to follow the river, with its prolific array of beacons for just

over two miles (3½ km) as it swings eastward around Upper Sands. The river embankment will take you all the way to Reedness where the 'de Redenesse' family seems to have once flourished and in 1287 were granted a licence for the building of a Chapel in the Manor of Reedness. In 1346 Sir William de Redenesse was granted 'pardon for his good service in the War of France for homicides, felonies, robberies and trespasses committed before September 4th last'. ↓

Another pardon in 1386 was granted to John Elmsall, a servant of Thomas de Redenesse, for the murder of John Mundson of Swynflete.

Reedness seems in later centuries to have enjoyed some prominence as a landing and ferry crossing. There was a price to be paid for this. In 1633 Lord Wentworth (who was to become Earl of Strafford and beheaded by Parliament's command in 1641) wrote to tell London that 'Pestilence has come into divers parts of Co. York. Redness and Airmin are furiously infected and 100 persons dead, this being brought out of Lincolnshire … it was brought into the suburbs of York by a lewd woman from Airmin … the passages from Lincolnshire have been stopped as much as possible'.

Meanwhile the Admiralty Court's fining of Reedness in 1693 for not removing 'the piles and stumps of an old staith called King's Staith in the Constablery of Rednesse' suggests that sometime between 1633 and 1693 the wharf had closed down. Perhaps it never recovered from the plague.

Go forward through Whitgift – pronounced Wigift and from Whitgift Sewer, the path is way marked to Blacktoft Sands. → *page 118*

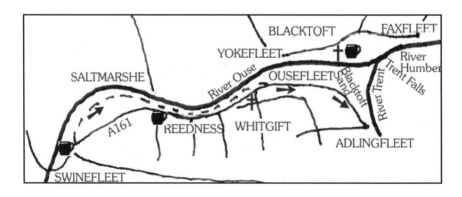

At Whitgift old red-brick houses cluster around the grey church sunk behind the high embankment protecting the rich warp land celebrated for the growth of potatoes and wheat. Here on this high causeway in 1690 Edward Mangall was gibbeted for the murder of Elizabeth Johnson and her illegitimate child.

Time is an important element in navigational calculations, but fortunately passing sailors do not have to depend on the whimsical

The clock on Whitgift church

clock of St Mary Magdalene Church. High up on its bell-tower and clearly visible from the river is the timepiece erected in 1919 with the Latin inscription 'Peace on Earth' – but no twelfth hour! Instead, it has number thirteen – a fact which the propagandist William Joyce, better known perhaps as 'Lord Haw-Haw', gleefully broadcast during the Second World War as evidence of the efficient German intelligence system. Local legend has it that the painter responsible for the Roman digits which mark the hours apparently passed much of his time in the adjacent Angel and Ferry Inn – formerly the ferry house and now a private dwelling – where he became somewhat bemused from imbibing too much ale. As a result he had to finish the job in a hurry and consequently painted the last number as XIII.

Since it is known there was a church here between AD1127 and 1137, the protective sea wall between the river and church was probably built by the monks of Selby before that date and a tidal sluice which must be the earliest known in the country. In the 1960s it was replaced by a thrust-bored pipe culvert with a tidal flap-valve.

It was while crossing Whitgift ferry on 3rd December 1614 that Sir John Sheffield (son of the then President of the Council of the North), his two brothers and servants were drowned. Their bodies were never recovered. An elegy about the tragedy was written by poet Michael Drayton, but he confused the Ouse with the Humber. Charles I used this ferry in 1642 when he moved from York to Nottingham to raise his standard at the beginning of the Civil War. A more frequent user was John Wesley, who made more than forty preaching visits around

Lighthouse at Ousefleet

Yorkshire from his beloved Epworth. According to his Journal, he seems to have had a particularly unpleasant crossing on Saturday, 19th May 1753. 'I preached at Pocklington again,' he writes, 'and rode on to Whitgift Ferry. It rained a great part of the way, and just as we got to the water a furious shower began, which continued above half an hour, while we were striving to get John Haime's horse into the boat; but we were forced after all to leave him behind ...'

In August 1859, Whitgift Ferry was advertising 'Excellent accommodation now offered for conveying passengers, cattle, horses and gigs across the Ouse'. The special cattle ferry could carry twenty-five beasts.

The ferry landing has gone, a victim of twentieth-century bank improvements, and the 'day boats' which enabled the villagers to go shopping in Hull for a return fare of eight pence are no more than a fond memory. So too are the paddle-steamers which ran popular day trips to Spurn, Whitton, Grimsby and Ferriby.

The river is constantly widening now as you walk forward along the embankment to Ousefleet, where a lighthouse warns of the hazard of Whitgift Ness mud and sandbanks. Giant pylons bestride the river to lift National Grid electricity cables high in the air, exaggerating the Lilliputian impression of surroundings.

From now on also the path can be very overgrown all the way to Blacktoft Sands. When you enter the RSPB conservation land, just before the pylons near Ousefleet, the path follows the embankment on its right hand side ↓

Flooding was once a common misfortune so land drainage and protective earthworks has always been a priory hereabouts. Consequently it was the task of priests and landlords of bygone days – people who were generally known by the name of the place where they were born – to maintain such banks as existed. It was this never ceasing work that has left us the records of men such as Roger de Hoveden, John de Huck, John de Armin, and Gerard de Useflete. In the reigns of Edward I and Edward II the names of both Gerard de Useflete and Loretta, the wife of John Useflete are mentioned as people responsible for 'viewing' the banks of the river while in 1325 Edward II appointed Thomas de Howke to survey the banks of the River Ouse and twenty years later Sir William Rednesse carried out a survey near Rawcliffe.

Only another mile (1½ km) separates you from Blacktoft Sand washed by Blacktoft Channel where you find the RSPB Humber Wild Fowl Refuge adored by bird-watchers who come to observation hides to view some of the 100,000 or so pink-footed geese and other wildfowl that wing their way annually to these mudflats as they migrate.

Once you enter the area of the reserve through a gate, the path continues on the right of the bank and brings you to the access road to the RSPB reception. (You must pay to visit the reserve unless a member of the RSPB). → *page 120*

A century ago this silt-laden river was a treacherous place of shifting shoals, sandbanks and saltings a mile and a quarter wide (2 km). And the Ouse was divided into a north and a south channel by Blacktoft Island.

But during the 1920s and 30s massive civil engineering works confined the waters to much narrower channels by a system of 'stoned training walls'. As a result the Ouse now flows through what was the north channel, while Blacktoft Island, plus the south channel, became a 'cut-off', silted up and developed as a the reed bed extension of the land we see today.

Around 1,700 pink-footed geese arrive here for the winter and on the ground they are ordinary creatures but once in the sky they seem to assume a mystery which has always captured the imagination. Our ancestors shuddered in their beds when they heard the cries of geese overhead in the night.

'Gabriel hounds' they were called, or 'gabble rachets'. Gabriel was of course the angel of death and the unearthly cry of geese on the wing sometimes sounds like a pack of hounds. One of the myths about them said that wild geese were the souls of unbaptised children wandering the air until the day of judgement.

Stately shelducks, with their sealing-wax red bills, dunlin, ruff, oyster catcher, plovers, godwits, redshank and even curlews are attracted to this estuarine habitat of shallow, muddy lagoons and islands to feed on tiny crabs, snails, lugworms, sand hoppers, shrimps, and shelled molluscs like cockles. Tightly packed flocks of these waders take off in a smokey smudge that sways and swerves, twists and turns with high speed acrobatics, before descending in perfect echelons of flashing white wings to dibble and delve in the mud for tasty morsels.

Beyond the lagoons stretch the vast reed beds that glow a warm parchment-gold in the sun, gradually darkening to a soft buff brown in the distance. These dense, impenetrable reed beds are the home of large numbers of reed warblers and bearded tits, reed buntings and sedge warblers, as well as short-eared owls. Marsh harriers often put in an appearance too. Ornithological highlights include the autumn swallow roost – 75,000 strong – and the wintering Scandinavian hen harriers. Even avocets have been known to drop in but above all else it is the great shelduck production factory of Yorkshire,

You can make your journey's end here if you wish, but you cannot see the river that you have been following for so long, despite the confluence of the Ouse and Trent at Trent Falls being so close in the parish of Adlingfleet. Consequently the vision of the Ouse that was born incognito ends in obscurity.

To get closer to the confluence cross the access road and walk just over 2km (1.5 miles) along the public right of way down to the inlet crossing at Adlingfleet Ings. Just before the path bends south on the left bank is an iron post recording the lower limit of improvements works carried out by the Aire & Calder Navigation Company in 1886. Look left from Adlingfleet Ings and you get a good view of the River Trent at Trent Falls entering Whitton Channel with the Ouse alongside.

To see the Ouse individually entering Whitton Channel you would need to visit Blacktoft and Faxfleet on the opposite bank, for Faxfleet marks more clearly the confluence of the Ouse with the Trent through the dangerous rapids somewhat grandiloquently known as Trent Falls.

Unfortunately the view there does not now coincide with that of the Vicar of Owston Ferry who in 1836 observed: 'all is bustle and animation on the river: some vessels immediately prepare to resume their voyage to Gainsborough, while others get all things in readiness against the reflux of the stream in order to avail themselves of deep water for their passage to the Humber. Then comes the steam packet from Hull on its daily voyage to Gainsborough; passengers are landed and embarked; and if the wind be favourable as the tide continues to flow, brigs, schooners, sea sloops and keels pass in rapid succession so that on a fine summer's morning or evening at which time from six to nine-o'clock, the spring tides in this part of the river always flow, the sight is truly animating and delightful'.

At Blacktoft the choppy waters of the river top the last few feet of rotting timbers that formed the first jetty built just over a century ago at the isolated hamlet. Nearby is the massive new concrete replacement opened in 1956. The original jetty, inclusive of land, cost about £3,500, but it proved so popular that in 1881 a further £2,064 was spent on an extension. Blacktoft jetty has been, and still is, a godsend to mariners using the lower Ouse, for without it many a vessel would have grounded on Whitton Sands just below Trent Falls or would have had to delay departure until there was enough water to carry them over other shoals.

Although built as a temporary mooring to safeguard craft from grounding, unloading of vessels has occasionally been sanctioned, a practice about which the Customs authorities did not enthuse, since it clearly afforded opportunities for smuggling. In 1888 the local Customs officer reported on 17th February:.

'The pier at Blacktoft ... is a place where grave mischief might possibly break out at any time. It cannot be visited from Goole with sufficient frequency or with the possibility of adequate results accruing ... Three

or four steamers at a time inward bound from dangerous continental Ports, often lie at this pier for a whole night during neap tides – during the prevalence of fogs even longer – and outward-bound vessels, with stores from Bond on board, are often obliged to stop here on their way down the River from the same causes'.

His masters clearly heeded his words, and from 1888 to 1892 they posted a permanent Customs officer there to discourage nefarious activities on dark nights and in foggy weather

To this day Blacktoft jetty is invaluable to vessels late on their tide and to coasters that have come downstream from Selby or Goole. Here they lie, hostage to the river, hemmed in by Blacktoft Sand and the long, low banks covered by huge reeds, some of which are six or seven feet (2 metres) high but still within reach of the very highest tides.

Adjacent is the Hope & Anchor inn *which doubtless proves to be an inviting beacon for passers-by whether afloat or ashore.*

The Hope & Anchor Inn at Blacktoft

Blacktoft seems to have usurped adjacent Faxfleet for the role of nautical lay-by. Proof comes from a royal document signed at Oudenarde on 5th September 1339. (King Edward III was campaigning in Flanders against the French; it was the beginning of the Hundred Years' War), giving the merchants of York permission to send their woollen hides, on which export duties had to be paid, by 'little ships' to Selby and Faxfleet 'when the great ships on account of too shallow water, cannot get to their fair city'. Furthermore two Roman brooches – one in enamel dragonesque style nearly two inches long –

found on the banks here in 1965 lend support to the view that there existed a thriving Romano-British community, partly agricultural, partly making pottery, with its own little harbour which probably served a much wider area. For many years Faxfleet was a recognized port of call and even warranted a market and fair. Seemingly neither port nor market enjoyed much success, for local families diverted their shipping-interests down river, like John de Faxfleet who in 1305 'sailed from the port of Hull with seventeen loads of lead, scarlet cloth of Lincolnshire, cheese and salmon', and William de Faxfleet who somewhat later played a lively and profitable part in the affairs of Barton-on-Humber. Only the old approach to the river bank at the end of Faxfleet Lane now identifies the staith where the 'little ships' tied up and transferred their cargo to 'the great ships' – the sturdy cogs and busses which could withstand the buffetings of the North Sea.

See box on page 124

Born high on Biddulph Moor in the northern corner of Staffordshire near Thursfield, the River Trent might reasonably be expected to pour itself into the Irish Sea some 30 miles west. But the newborn river yields to the surrounding hills and moor to descend over 300 feet (91 metres) in its first four miles (6 ½ km) as it flows for over 170 miles (274 km) through four counties, greedily picking up streams on the way to bequeath them all to another. On the way it drains more than two and a half million acres. Edmund Spenser says the Trent owes its name to having 'both thirty sorts of fish and thirty sundry streames', but this elegiac explanation hardly stands scrutiny. More likely the name is of Celtic origin, being a contracted form of `Derwent`, meaning 'river where oaks are common'.

The two united rivers now forfeit identities to the broader reaches of the Humber, some two miles (3km) in width as it floods over Whitton Sand towards the great Humber suspension bridge, heading for even more open waters, for as Ecclesiastes reminds us: 'All the rivers run into the sea.'

Refuge for Royalty?

The decline of Faxfleet seems all the more peculiar considering that on at least three occasions in the Middle Ages the rural tranquillity was ruffled by the arrival of a reigning monarch. On 18th April 1303 Edward I was there on his way to the shrine of St John at Beverley to invoke success for a new campaign. The unlucky Edward II spent nearly a month at Faxfleet in July 1323, less than four years before he lost his crown. And during one of his frequent visits to Yorkshire Henry IV visited Faxfleet on 8th September 1407.

Why did they come? Where did they stay? What did they do? The tantalizing queries go on and on – largely unanswered. Is there a relic in the name of a field called King's Close? Back Lane leading into Faxfleet Lane is named as King Street in the Manor Court Rolls of 1745. This, at least, seems to have been a recognized highway, and along the same route was King's Staith at Blacktoft.

Did they come to dispense justice? We know that in 1351 a case was brought before the King by Lewis, Bishop of Durham, who, on his way home from Parliament held in the previous year, had been shipwrecked in the Ouse and lost his baggage. 'The men of Faxfleet,' he claimed, were among the beach-combers who carried off his possessions, 'and they detain them yet'.

And in 1362 the Faxfleet ferrymen, along with those at Whitgift, were in trouble for overcharging – 'one penny for the crossing when they ought to take one halfpenny'.

Edward II came to Faxfleet after hunting in the Forest of Galtres, north of York. Whilst here he managed to transact a considerable volume of administrative tasks, including drawing up at least thirty-two letters together with as many writs and charters. The scene seems hardly credible. Peasants in the meadows harvesting the last of the hay, mariners manoeuvring vessels up and down the changing river, milkmaids bringing in the cattle – and in the midst of it all the monarch busy with the affairs of his realm. Picture him instructing the clerks to write to the Dean and Chapter of Wells remonstrating with them for acquiring land without royal licence; to the bailiffs of Cumberland insisting on passports for all travellers from north of the border; to the justices in London over the dispute about a ship belonging to Coventry and robbed by Portsmouth men as it came from France; and directing the Dublin justices to be more diligent in enforcing the King's prerogative in that uncertain part of his realm.

Perhaps a more obvious explanation for the choice of Faxfleet to enjoy the distinction of royal patronage lies in its location at the junction of a river system – a useful place to take ship either across or down the Humber, up the Trent or up the Ouse.

More books from Meridian...

BEYOND THE BARS: Ten Walks from York City Wallsby Ivan E Broadhead

Circular walks into the countryside and villages surrounding York, ranging in distance from two to seven miles and starting from the ten historic exits from the city walls.

£5.95. ISBN 1 869922 05 0. 192 pages. 84 photographs. 10 maps.

WATERSIDE WALKS IN NORTH YORKSHIRE by Ivan E Broadhead

Twenty walks, featuring brooks, streams, canals, waterfalls, lakes, rivers and the sea, in one of Britains most beautiful counties.

Revised second edition £5.95. ISBN 978-1 869922 55 9. 96 pages. 32 photographs. 20 maps.

DISCOVERY WALKS AROUND THE WELSH BORDERS by Brian Conduit

The Welsh Border counties possess some of the most delightful ancient towns in the country. The villages are unspoiled and the fine countryside has grand views and some mighty castles.

The twenty splendid walks here are well within the capabilities of the average walker, ranging between 3½ and 8 miles. Good pubs and places of refreshment are noted, and most of the walks are accessible by public transport.

£5.95. ISBN-13: 978-1-869922-58-0 86 pages. 42 b/w photos. 20 sketch maps.

COUNTRY WALKS AROUND THE NATIONAL FOREST by Brian Conduit

The National Forest is an area of 200 square miles covering parts of Leicestershire, Staffordshire and Derbyshire. This collection of twenty walks is not just confined to the boundaries of the National Forest but also includes a number of interesting and attractive areas on its periphery. Among the major attractions are the many woodlands, both new and mature, paths across riverside meadows and along canal towpaths, attractive villages, great parklands, and many sites of historic interest.

£5.95. ISBN 978-1-869922-56-6. 84 pages. 37 illustrations. 20 maps

BEST WALKS IN THE MIDLANDS by Des Wright

This is the fourth collection of walks prepared by Des Wright, an author with a passionate life-long interest in the countryside and its wildlife. Each of the twenty walks has been designed with a specific focus – such as an unusual or notable building, a unique pub, a church with a fine spire, a folly, a natural object or an impressive view.

The walks are not difficult and are well within the capabilities of the average walker. Some are quite short and others have shorter options and so will appeal to those with young families or those who are taking their first steps in exploring the 'great outdoors'. The distances range from 3½ miles to 12 miles. Most can be accessed by public transport and details of suitable services are provided.

£6.95. ISBN-13: 978-1-869922-57-3 120 pages. 38 b/w photos. 20 sketch maps.

RAMBLERS' CHOICE: Some favourite walks in the Midlands Edited by Peter Groves

In this collection members of the City of Birmingham Group of the Ramblers' Association offer some of their favourite walks in Warwickshire, West Midlands, Worcestershire and Staffordshire. They are not too difficult and many have longer and shorter versions, the longer walks ranging from about 5 miles/8km to 9½ miles/15 km; the shorter walks from about 3 miles/5 km to 7¾ miles/12.5 km.

£5.95. ISBN 978-1-869922-54-2. 96 pages. 31 illustrations. 20 maps

HERITAGE DISCOVERY WALKS IN THE MIDLANDS by Peter Groves

Britain has a rich historical heritage and the twenty-one walks in this book explore some fine Midlands countryside with opportunities to visit castles, battlefields, nature reserves, museums, churches and cathedrals, to admire fine architecture and to explore some historic towns. The walks range from 2½ miles/4km to 11¼ miles/18 km.

£6.95. ISBN 1-869922-50-6. 160 pages. 52 illustrations. 20 maps

A YEAR OF WALKS IN THE THREE CHOIRS COUNTIES by Roy Woodcock

The Three Choirs Counties comprise Herefordshire, Gloucestershire and Worcestershire and this selection of walks takes twelve widely distributed locations, one for each month of the year. Each walk is described for a particular month, but all of them are good for any time of the year. Each location provides two walks (or occasionally three) giving about a couple of hours of gentle walking: these can be joined together to provide longer walks.

£6.95. ISBN 1-869922-51-4. 112 pages. 28 illustrations. 12 maps

WALKS IN SEVERN COUNTRY by Roy Woodcock

The River Severn, Britain's longest river, rises in Wales and flows through the beautiful counties of Powys, Shropshire, Worcestershire and Gloucestershire before discharging into the Bristol Channel. In this book the author presents an absorbing account of the geography and history of the river accompanied by twenty walks that explore some of the fine towns and countryside that the Severn passes through on its 220 mile journey to the sea.

£7.95. ISBN 1-869922-49-2. 128 pages. 37 illustrations. 20 maps

WARWICKSHIRE WALKS TO WET YOUR WHISTLE by Roger Seedhouse

Following his two highly successful books, Walks to Wet your Whistle and More Walks to Wet your Whistle, Roger Seedhouse now presents a further collection of walks, all with good pubs, in Warwickshire – a land of lakes and country parks which are a delight to behold, merging into the Northern Cotswolds with its buildings of honey-hued stone.

£8.95. ISBN 1-869922-48-4 120 pages 21 photos 20 maps

WALKS IN WARWICKSHIRE AND WORCESTERSHIRE A Third Collection by Des Wright

This third collection of walks by a popular author explores further some of the attractive countryside in two West Midlands counties. The walking is not difficult, mostly on the flat and with no strenuous climbs. The walks are all circular and can be reached easily by car and, with one exception, by public transport. Distances range between 2 and 9.5 miles, with one rather more strenuous walk of l4 miles.

£6.95. ISBN 1-869922-44-1. 112 pages. 24 illustrations. 22 maps.

A TEME VALLEY WALK by David Milton

The Teme is one of the most beautiful and fast-flowing rivers in the country but remains quite secretive for much of its length. This long distance walk remains as close as possible to the river but takes to the hills where footpaths, public transport or accommodation needs dictate. It starts in Worcester and ends, after visiting the source of the river, in Newtown, a total distance of 93 miles.

£8.95. ISBN 1-869922-45-X. 176 pages. 22 illustrations. 17 maps.

THE RIVERSIDES WAY by David Milton

A 70 mile circular walk in the area of the Welsh Marches immediately to the south and west of Ludlow. Centred on Aymestry it takes in the valleys and surrounding hills of the two rivers that drain the region – the Teme, in the north, and the Lugg, in the south.

£8.95. ISBN 1-869922-43-3. 160 pages. 13 photos. 14 maps.

WALKS THROUGH HISTORY IN THE HEART OF ENGLAND by Roger Seedhouse

The Heart of England is rich in history, both ancient and more modern, and the twenty-four walks in this book will offer the enquiring walker many intriguing glimpses of a bygone age – with iron-age forts, battle sites, medieval castles and even a second world war camp. All of them start at, or pass through, places of historical interest that will add greatly to your appreciation of a day out in beautiful walking country.

£8.95 ISBN 1-869922-41-7. 160 pages. 38 photos. 24 maps.

THE ELAN VALLEY WAY by David Milton

The Elan Valley Way runs from Frankley, on the western fringe of Birmingham, to the Elan Valley in mid-Wales. It is loosely based around the course followed by the Elan Valley aqueduct along which Birmingham's water supply has passed since 1904. Largely following footpaths and bridleways, and with many superb views, the 128½ mile route passes through some delightful walking areas in the counties of Worcestershire, Shropshire, Herefordshire and Powys.

£7.95. ISBN 1 869922 39 5. 160 pages. 21 photographs. 21 maps.

WALKS IN SOUTH WARWICKSHIRE
FROM SHAKESPEARE COUNTRY TO THE COTSWOLDS by John W Pamham and Barry R Wills

This collection of circular walks represent the authors' favourites within this lovely, varied region. The walks will take you along ancient trackways and paths, past standing stones, earthworks, country estates and grand houses. In the Arden countryside as well as finding connections to William Shakespeare you will discover hidden valleys and distinct wooded hilltops that offer wonderful views. Further south the walks will take you through delightful villages and into remote areas in the Cotswold Hills that rival in many ways the better known parts of this beautiful region.

£6.95. ISBN 1 869922 38 7. 112 pages. 36 sketches. 18 maps.

THE MONARCH'S WAY by Trevor Antill

A long distance walk that closely follows the route taken by Charles II after his defeat by Cromwell's forces at Worcester in 1651. Starting from Worcester it goes through the Cotswolds and the Mendips to the coast, then along the South Downs to Shoreham where Charles escaped to France. Visiting many historic places, perhaps previously known to readers only through the history books, it also goes through some of the finest scenery in western and southern England.

Book 1: Worcester to Stratford-upon-Avon. 180 miles.Revised second edition £6.95. ISBN 1 869922 52 2. 112 pages. 19 photographs, 8 drawings, 19 maps.

Book 2: Stratford-upon-Avon to Charmouth. 210 miles.£6.95. ISBN 1 869922 28 X. 136 pages. 21 photographs. 23 maps.

Book 3: Charmouth to Shoreham. 225 miles.£6.95. ISBN 1 869922 29 8. 136 pages. 21 photographs. 25 maps.

THE NAVIGATION WAY: A Hundred Mile Towpath Walk by Peter Groves and Trevor Antill

Starting from the centre of Birmingham and encompassing fourteen West Midlands canals the Navigation Way follows a meandering course through varied urban areas and delightful countryside until terminating at Chasewater. Now again revised to cover the many changes and improvements that have been made to the towpaths its twelve sections provide a series of walks ranging from 5¼ to 11 miles. The book also contains ten additional circular 'canal-link' walks in some of the attractive walking areas adjacent to the canals.

Third revised edition.£5.95. ISBN 1 869922 35 2. 112 pages. 34 photographs. 24 maps.

WALKS AROUND THE MALVERNS by Roy Woodcock

The Malvern Hills and their surroundings provide magnificent opportunities for rambling, and in this book of twenty walks Roy Woodcock explores many of their superb features. The walks cover the entire range of hills and the neighbouring commons, together with some of the delightful countryside nearby.

Second revised edition £6.95. ISBN 1 869922 53 0. 112 pages. 41 illustrations. 20 maps.

WALKS TO WET YOUR WHISTLE by Roger Seedhouse

Eighteen walks covering some of the most beautiful countryside in Shropshire and along its Staffordshire borders, each providing an opportunity to visit a pub in which the walker will feel welcome and comfortable. The main walks range in distance between 7 and 11½ miles but each has a shorter alternative of between 2¾ and 5¼ miles.

£6.95. ISBN 1 869922 41 7. 112 pages. 17 photographs. 18 maps.

MORE WALKS TO WET YOUR WHISTLE by Roger Seedhouse

Following the author's highly successful first book he now presents a second collection of walks with a pub in Shropshire and along its Staffordshire borders.

£6.95. ISBN 1 869922 36 0. 112 pages. 24 photographs. 18 maps.

WATERSIDE WALKS IN THE MIDLANDS
by Birmingham Ramblers: edited by Peter Groves

Twenty-two walks featuring brooks, streams, pools, rivers and canals. Some can be found a short distance from the centre of Britain's second city; others will take the reader further afield in the West Midlands and into the attractive counties of Warwickshire, Worcestershire, Shropshire, Staffordshire and Derbyshire.

£4.95. ISBN 1 869922 09 3. 112 pages. 28 photographs. 22 maps.

MORE WATERSIDE WALKS IN THE MIDLANDS
by Birmingham Ramblers: edited by Peter Groves

Following on the success of their first book, *Waterside Walks in the Midlands*, members of the City of Birmingham Branch of the Ramblers' Association have now prepared another collection on a similar theme. As before, the walks feature brooks, streams, rivers, canals and pools - sometimes as a major aspect of a walk, sometimes as a feature to encounter as you ramble through some of the fine Midlands countryside. Distances range from 4½ miles to14 miles.

£5.95. ISBN 1 869922 31 X. 112 pages. 21 photographs. 18 maps. Paperback. A5.

All Meridian titles are available from booksellers or direct from the publishers.
Please send your remittance, including the following amounts for postage and packing:
Order value up to £10.00 add £1.50;
over £10.00 and up to £20.00 add £2.00;
over £20.00 add £2.50.

Meridian Books
8 Hartside Close, Lutley, Halesowen, West Midlands B63 1HP
Tel: 0121-429 4397; e-mail: meridian.books@tiscali.co.uk